CELEBRATION OF STEAM

West Midlands

J. B. Bucknall

IAN ALLAN Publishing

First published 1994

ISBN 0 7110 2250 X

Published by Ian Allan Publishing

an imprint of Ian Allan Ltd, Terminal House,
Station Approach, Shepperton, Surrey TW17 8AS;
and printed by Ian Allan Printing Ltd,
Coombelands House, Coombelands Lane,
Addlestone, Weybridge, Surrey KT15 1HY.

Title page:
**The original Birmingham Moor Street station was closed on
26 September 1987. The day was commemorated by the use of
Tyseley's preserved No 7029 *Clun Castle* on a special service to
Knowle and Dorridge. '2MT' 2-6-0 No 46443 was also a participant
in the proceedings. The headboard on the smokebox of the 'Castle'
was appropriate to the occasion, well drafted and with obviously
sentimental overtones: 'Farewell to Old Moor St'.** *Mike Wood*

Below:
**Atherstone station owed much of its charm to its unusual signalbox
situated between the fast lines, expresses virtually speeding below
the box in both directions. With the signalman looking on, No 45737
Atlas was about to depart with the 1.45pm Liverpool-Rugby
semi-fast on 23 May 1961.** *Hugh Ballantyne*

Front cover:
**'Castle' No 5070 *Sir Daniel Gooch* pictured in front of the coaling
stage at Stafford Road Shed.**

Back cover top:
**Stanier Pacific No 46245 *City of London* heads
towards Wolverhampton High Level with
stock from the carriage sidings.**

Back cover lower:
**Class 9F No 92130 stands at Stafford Shed, with
the station in the background** *All J.B. Bucknall*

Contents

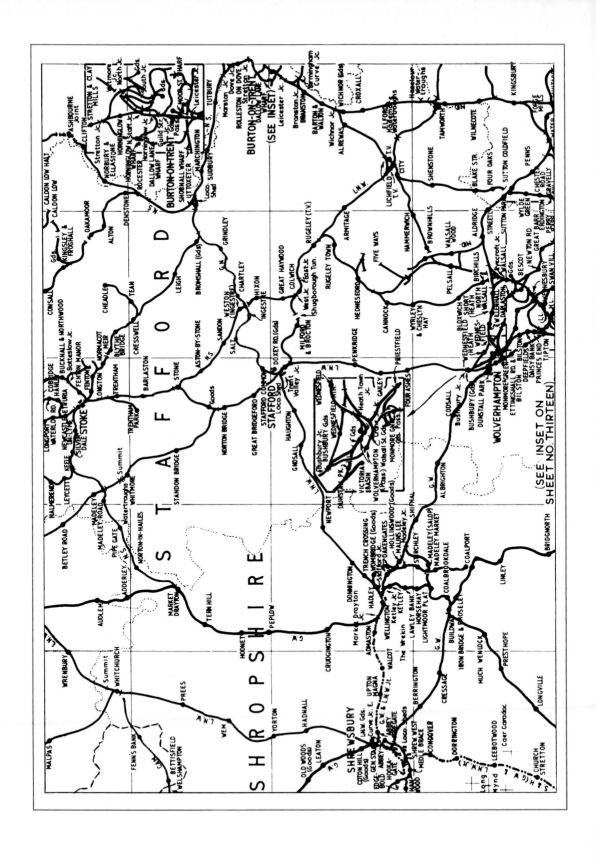

Foreword

When invited to compile this volume, one of the first in a series of Ian Allan albums depicting the late steam era on Britain's railways, I was aware of getting a quart into a pint pot. The outline remit required about 250 photographs to portray steam operations in the north West Midlands — an area in part dynamic, varied and highly populated, but also with huge tracts of forest, undulating farmland, market towns and picturesque villages. The task would not be simple with 1,000 photographs, so at best this volume can only be a sampler of the complex railway system within the Midlands area, which, for the purposes of this book, can be defined as that area bounded by Birmingham, Burton upon Trent, Crewe and Shrewsbury.

With over 1,000 locomotives based in the area, plus those passing through, the small industrial 0-4-0T was just as critically honed to its humble duties as the crack Pacific. While balance has been desirable, it has not been allowed to dominate completely. The main routes, their infrastructure and steam locomotives have featured in many other published works, while many branch lines and industrial locations have not. I am deeply indebted to my friends and fellow cameramen who have made available their priceless 'celluloid time capsules'. I too have shared and appreciated their patience and frustration during endless hours of lineside vigil, the vagaries of wind and weather, with plans often ended by yet another 'Atlantic low'.

Principal contributions have been made by Hugh Ballantyne, Geoff Bannister, Simon Dewey, John Ellson, Jack Haddock, Jim Hardy, Brian Robbins and Mike Wood with all unattributed photographs taken by the author. Others have made perhaps lesser contributions, yet other photographs have been purchased, handed on or otherwise procured, their origins unfortunately impossible to trace and are acknowledged therefore as from a contributor's collection. It is also necessary to acknowledge the co-operation, over many years, of the engine crews, station and depot staff, signalmen and management for permits and permission to photograph widely.

Likewise, thanks are due to their counterparts in the industrial field, especially to the management at Littleton colliery where closure has just been announced and where I have been made welcome over 35 years. Without their generosity, consideration, flexibility and trust, photographic volumes such as this would not have been possible. The easy going relationship soon forged with Peter Waller of Ian Allan Ltd ensured that the 'nitty-gritty' has been minimal, finalised informally over a coffee or two.

Since these pictures were taken over 25 years ago, much of the 'old' railway has vanished. Brake vans are virtually no more, automatic signalling systems have replaced signalboxes and track has been rationalised. The electrification of the West Coast main line eliminated cast-iron Victorian stations and their classic platform furniture. We hope that you will enjoy turning back the clock a little to the days of steam, elegance and charm, when a passing locomotive demanded attention and evoked an emotional response with sight, hearing and smell.

The generosity of Malcolm Woolhead (M&G Jaguar Spares & Restoration) of Four Ashes, Staffordshire, is acknowledged for help in photocopying text. I am indebted to my friend Harry Pratt, formerly Chief Traction Inspector (London Midland) and Traction/Driver Manager (InterCity Wolverhampton), for technical advice and reading through this manuscript.

John Bucknall
Stafford
January 1994

Above:
When steam was 'King' at Snow Hill. *Simon Dewey*

Introduction

The early railway locomotive proved to men of vision and money to have great potential for long-distance transportation of people, raw materials and manufactured goods. Speed, power and reliability in service were potentially almost limitless, and canal economics were soon to be eclipsed and doomed. Transport by road had to await the petrol and diesel engines and the terrific investment in the infrastructure of the motorway age until it would prove a real threat. Rail was to become king.

Rapidly developing rail networks served the needs of the country areas, town, city and manufacturing industries alike, and gave easy outlet to ports for worldwide trade. The heartland of Britain was but hours from the sea, days from the world. British locomotives, simple, robust and long-lived were to be seen throughout the world, developing continents, economies, lifestyles and needs as the railways conquered all. British-built was synonymous with quality.

At home, diversity within a common design framework produced a Swindon look at variance with a rival Premier Line. Locomotives designed for all types of service appeared in a startling array of in-house colours, liveries and adornments. Company aesthetics mirrored mechanical variation within the broad spectrum of functional design. Green, black, crimson, blue and even 'yellow' locomotives went about their similar tasks with variance in style, verve and panache. Difference was not only visual. The ear was wooed by whistle, bellow, wail or blare, while some Eastern locomotives 'peeped' like very reserved and refined robins.

There were subtle goodlookers. Others, though efficient and functional, could be considered ugly. Some designs were workmanlike, receiving the appellation 'the engineman's friend', others were reputed to be bad steamers and workshy. Some were specific to a speed range, power or duty,

others were all-rounders with a do-anything, go-anywhere capability. Locomotives in the public limelight were streamlined, some 'air smoothed', and 'Duchesses', like erring vicars, were 'defrocked'.

Comparisons between locomotives were at least hazardous, perhaps impossible. The 'best' was never acknowledged by consensus, judgement being coloured by prejudice, experience, and often by where you lived. The BR Standard types, well-researched and designed after consultation with experienced traincrews regarding cab layout and detail along with other home comforts, were never universally accepted. Western men still preferred to stand; and 'Britannias' were driven from the wrong side anyway! 'Number 7 back' was another 'Britannia' ailment of Western firemen, the only remedy being a return to a 'Castle' footplate with a firedoor at 'the correct height'. To me the 'Clan' Pacifics were to be regarded as incompetent after '009' had slipped itself to a standstill on leaving Stafford with a mediocre load for the south, while my adored 'Scots' and 'Patriots' would walk away with '16 on' day in and day out.

The north West Midlands had great variety in its locomotive fleets servicing the area, from the vintage to the modern, with Midland, LNWR and Great Western power, together with the designs of an ex-Western CME on the LMS all being seen in the area. Development and experiment continued in late steam days in the quest for better steaming and running efficiency. Poppet valve gears, self-cleaning smokeboxes, roller-bearings and rocking grates were perfected in service. 'Jubilee' double-chimney boilers rotated (*Connaught* and *Bahamas*), '8Fs' and 'Jubilees' exchanged small side-rail fitted tenders, while 'Patriots' and '4Fs' vied for tenders of the high, straight-sided variety. Supposedly standard classes were far from standard; compare the rivet detail of the

Above:
Typical of steam in its last decade, 'Hall' class No. 6925
***Hackness Hall* appears in carework condition.** *Simon Dewey*

'Princess Royal' Pacifics. All made for variety and interest.

During the 1950s and 1960s we were fortunate to witness steam at its zenith, but also at its crossroads, with steam power deemed outmoded and outdated as diesel and electric efficiency were compelling to a modern railway seemingly run by and for accountants and economists. Newly-built steam locomotives with years of efficient operation before them were to be axed to develop a 'modern' railway, where millions were squandered on untried diesel designs instead of selecting products of proven pedigree and service record. Scottish Bo-Bos became expensive 'Boo-Boos', while Clayton Type 1s were to become the shortest-lived 'standard class' ever. The quality machine was to be the big-engined, slow-running diesel-electric; the diesel-hydraulics did not stand the pace.

In the West Midlands, and throughout the country, the diesel and the DMU era took over quickly, often a single diesel replacing two or three steam locomotives. Storage space for withdrawn locomotives was at a premium, and quiet backwaters on the rail system were utilised as holding areas prior to sale and dispersal, as steam was doomed to the scrapman's torch.

However, some groups, led by men of vision, were determined to retain a steam heritage for future generations — the preservation movement was born. The author became associated with the Gresley Society (despite being an outright Stanier man!) — probably through the persuasion of Keith Pirt and others. The intention was to preserve No 60103. Enthusiasts in preservation were, at that time, few, with money scarce and hard-earned by the mass production of saleable postcards by the thousand, jumble sales, slide lectures, and other means. Other societies had other objectives and so a representative steam collection was saved, added to later as the 'National Collection' became a reality. An 'A3' could be purchased for £3,000 or so, smaller locomotives for less. Colleagues in the industrial steam field likewise earmarked unique and interesting locomotives for preservation. These can now be seen at, among other places, Chasewater, Shackerstone and Foxfield. Well-worn and tired machinery was lovingly restored to full working standard.

As I write these notes, Littleton colliery, with the generous co-operation of its management and locomotive staff, is holding a running weekend with visiting 'Austerities' *Whiston* and *Wimblebury* from Foxfield reviving memories of the busy working colliery of 20 or so years ago, when there was an extensive steam locomotive fleet for coal distribution to the main line at Penkridge. Steam was considered to be economically dead, but its resurrection has thankfully been thorough and permanent. Coal smoke, oil and steam are still a potent blend for the steam enthusiast. Ethereal, whispy, enigmatic steam, or jet black 'clag' blasted to the sky, the breath of a living, vibrant, but gentle monster is still talked about, witnessed, photographed,

video-recorded or artistically represented. A rich heritage indeed.

For me, 'real' main line steam operations finished in 1968. To the end, superbly-designed steam locomotives struggled on with minimum maintenance and a common-use policy of manning. Gone were the days of selected coal for Class 1 workings. What went into the tender or bunker was what was available, varying from huge lumps to near power station 'slack', even lozenge-shaped brickettes.

Some locomotives rode rough, big-ends knocked and some 'V2s' produced some amazing offbeat syncopated Gresley music. Prodigious feats by the locomen, often unrecorded and unappreciated, were performed by crews coaxing along run-down machinery which in better days would have seen shops months before. 'Duchesses' still worked overnight Euston-Perth sleepers over the hills with anything up to '16 on', the superb Type 4 diesels (later Class 40s) being

Above:
Produced principally for suburban passenger duties, the Western 2-6-2Ts undertook a wide range of duties including the mixed freight featured here at work on Hatton Bank. The wide variety of stock hauled by such trains, the tanks and both steel and wooden-bodied wagons and vans of this con-sist, contrasted strongly with the company block trains to be **found on the railway in the 1990s. Churchward designed the '31xx' class in 1903, No 4125 (84D Leamington) being a later build of the 5ft 8in driving-wheeled tanks, which took the running numbers vacated by the withdrawal of Dean's older 4-4-0s of the 'Badminton', 'Atbara' and 'Flower' classes.**
Jim Hardy

considered underpowered for the job. The glamour days of steam were over, not just in Britain, but worldwide.

In Britain, workstained and grimy locomotives became the norm as a buoyant economy provided better paid jobs than railway work with its unsocial hours. But what could be done with the staff resources was done. Once the Modernisation Plan was agreed, the few locomotives visiting works came out unlined, or patch painted only, unlikely to be cleaned. For those who in general like work-stained, grimy locomotives with indecipherable numbers, I apologise, as many of the illustrations in this book depict, thankfully, locomotives in some decorum and dignity. I am very appreciative of the efforts of all the men who operated steam during its final days, up to its final day at Lostock Hall in 1968. There an all-out attempt was made to polish up the locomotives for the last rites. One '8F', not to be cleaned officially, went out for its final duties well rubbed over, and far from immaculate, but presentable due to the hard work of Bill Ashcroft, guiding light of the Preston branch of the RCTS, and myself. But that was 25 years ago. I can still smell those oily rags!

Above:
Photographed during a week operating Solihull locals before a final visit to Swindon, the driver of 'King' class 4-6-0 No 6018 *King Henry VI* was alert to the road ahead on what was a very spirited service with a load hardly likely to tax a 'King'. No 6018 (81A) was withdrawn in December 1962 along with fellow Old Oak Common shedmates Nos 6000, 6011 and 6025. No 6018 was cut up at Swindon. Several 'Kings' were similarly dealt with locally: No 6005 by Cashmores of Great Bridge; and Cox & Danks of Langley Green, Oldbury, torched Stafford Road's Nos 6001/7/12/14-17/20/22/27 together with Plymouth Laira's No 6002.
Jim Hardy

Around Birmingham

Birmingham area main line activity has been well documented, whereas the highly rewarding steam backwaters and their locomotives have never had the same exposure. Classic green locomotives at Snow Hill were daily in the public limelight, the hardworking little locomotives in industry never achieved their true recognition. The smelters and furnaces of the West Midlands painted the night sky with light, smoke and steam, also emitted a cacophony of sound, the song of press and mill. This background noise of generating wealth was interjected by the urgent exhausts of diminutive steam locomotives with lion hearts, themselves often under the hammer, dragging, lugging, shunting, often slipping under heavy load on steep gradient, joining in industry's symphonic rhapsody — a Music of the Night. A cross-section of such faithful little machines has achieved rest in museums; others, steaming on, are admired as respected senior citizens in more active preservation on systems throughout the Midlands or even further afield.

Above:
Before hauling an SLS special to Swindon as a grand finale to commemorate the work of the Collett 'Kings' since their introduction in 1927, No 6018 *King Henry VI* was used for a week of evening rush-hour Solihull commuter trains. This majestic portrait makes up for some of the sadness felt at the end of the reign of 'Kings' on Paddington-Wolverhampton services and over the principal Western routes throughout the country.
Jim Hardy

Above:
Snow Hill typified the unique and expansive charm of the principal main line Great Western station. An elaborate and ornate backcloth of blue brick panels, built on massive steel girders, complemented the classic lines of No 6007 *King William III*. A tender of coal brickettes was fronted by better quality coal nearer the footplate. The author had a particular affinity with things Western at Snow Hill; Uncle Alfred was second-in-charge there whilst Uncle Len passed through daily for many years as he was senior guard on the 'Paddingtons'.
All uncredited photographs are by the author

Right:
No 4079 *Pendennis Castle* worked the Ian Allan 'Birkenhead Flyer' on Saturday 4 March 1967 from Paddington to Birkenhead and return. The locomotive then travelled light engine to Didcot for stabling overnight. It travelled north to Tyseley on Sunday 5 March, joining a collection of preserved locomotives, including Nos 7029, 1638, 3442 and 5593, for an extended stay in the roundhouse where artist Terence Cuneo set to work on another masterpiece. On arrival, fireman Johnny Griffin stood back to admire his charge. At the time No 4079 was owned by Mike Higson of Roundhouse Books. Note the Tyseley infrastructure still intact, and the presence of the Tyseley breakdown train. *Mike Wood*

Right:
GWR 0-6-0PT No 1638, formerly of Croes Newydd depot (Wrexham), had been purchased by Pat Whitehouse, Patrick Garland and John Trounson for use on the Dart Valley Railway. Restoration had been carried out prior to departure in the Tyseley workshops, which adjoined the roundhouse, where No 1638 was photographed on 5 March 1967. The '16xxs' were introduced by Hawksworth in 1949 for light branch line and shunting duties. *Mike Wood*

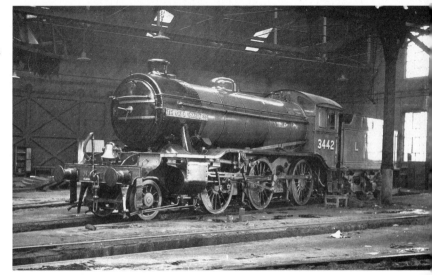

Right:
LNER 'K4' three-cylinder 2-6-0 No 3442 was designed by Gresley in 1937 as one of a class of six locomotives built for Scottish lines where a high tractive effort was required from a weight-restricted locomotive. *The Great Marquess,* **complete with bell, was photographed at Tyseley on 5 March 1967. It was then the property of Viscount Garnock; it is now based on the Severn Valley Railway.** *Mike Wood*

Right:
Class 5 4-6-0 No 44680 of Crewe South depot worked an SLS special train from Tyseley to Birkenhead to commemorate the decline of the former GWR main line from Paddington to Birkenhead as a through route. No 44680 made an explosive start from Tyseley, leaving in a cloud of steam and with considerable noise. No 7029 *Clun Castle* **also made the return journey to Birkenhead on 4 and 5 March 1967.** *Mike Wood*

Above:
Peckett 'Greenhythe' class (W6 Special) 0-6-0ST No 2058 of 1944 was photographed at the West Midlands Gas Board's Windsor Street Works, Birmingham, on 29 March 1969. Within three days of the photograph being taken No 3 could be seen awaiting its fate in Cashmore's scrapyard at Great Bridge. The dropped footplate of the classic little tank was necessitated by limited clearances at the site and the cab roof was little higher than the loaded wagons. Note the mechanical lubricator on the running plate. *Mike Wood*

Above:
R. & W. Hawthorn Leslie 0-4-0ST No 33 *Wellingborough No 3* (3813/1935) worked at Stewarts & Lloyds' Bromford Bridge tube works, Birmingham, where it shared duties on the internal rail traffic with Sentinel diesel *Barabel*. No 33 featured as motive power on 21 February 1970 hauling a train of empty bolster wagons from the storage sidings alongside the Derby-Birmingham ex-Midland main line into the works. In the background are plenty of stacked tubes awaiting departure. *Mike Wood*

Above:
Fort Dunlop rubber plant at Bromford Bridge, Birmingham, operated an internal railway system with a main line connection east of the former Bromford Bridge station. Steam operations ceased in 1970. In later years one of a fleet of three locomotives was rostered for daily use. The trio consisted of an ex-MOD Bagnall and two ex-CWS Irlam Pecketts. One of the latter, No 7 (2130/1951) is shown here on 18 January 1969 ambling back to its shed in typically filthy weather. All three locomotives survived into preservation. No 7 joined the fleet from Irlam in September 1966 and was preserved on withdrawal in 1971 when purchased by Hunts of Hinckley for the Market Bosworth Railway.
Mike Wood

Above:
W. G. Bagnall 0-6-0ST *Vulcan* (2994/1950) was recorded on film at rest inside the 'Top Shed' at the Longbridge Works of British Leyland on 18 January 1969. *Vulcan* was one of three locomotives of advanced design built for the Steel Company of Wales for comparison trials against equivalent diesels. The decision went in favour of the latter. Two of the Bagnalls were purchased for the Austin Motor Co in September 1957.
Mike Wood

15

Above:
Robert Stephenson & Hawthorn 0-6-0T No 3 (7537/1949) was parked alongside the wagon containing locomotive coal between duties at the CEGB Nechells power station on 7 March 1961. In the distance, against a backcloth of 'A' or Princes station, a Peckett 'W5' class 0-4-0ST (1438/1916) was hard at work drawing a train of empties round the curve and past the wooden cooling tower banks. The much taller and more modern concrete cooling tower of the newer Nechells 'B' power station can be seen emerging from the swirling steam of No 3 in the top right of the photograph.
Mike Wood

Above:
At the heart of the Nechells complex, RSH No 3 stood head to head (and inactive) with a Peckett 'W6' class 0-4-0ST (1478/1917) whilst RSH No 4 (7684/1951) had steam to spare while hauling a loaded coal train from Washwood Heath through the power station and into the already congested sidings. The locomotive fleet showed little standardisation in cabside numbering or warning 'tiger stripes' along the running plate edge.
Mike Wood

Above:
Viewed over the frozen canal on 21 February 1970, Nechells power station's locomotive depot commanded a central position within the complex and was overshadowed by the wooden cooling towers of 'A' station which dated back to 1916. Although they were no doubt considered modern for that year, and looking more suited for oast house or granary facilities, by this time they looked dated and outmoded. They were themselves dwarfed by the massive concrete construction of their counterparts within the more modern 'B' station. 'A' station gave reliable and continuous service over many years. *Mike Wood*

Above:
Willesden's allocation of pioneer main line diesels, Nos 10000/1 and 10201-3, was often employed on Wolverhampton services when not hauling express freight from the capital north to Basford Hall or Carlisle. With the Modernisation Plan well under way, the 'Duchesses' were available for duties away from the London-Carlisle/Glasgow route. With English Electric Type 4s working the Liverpool turns and the prototype diesels withdrawn, Nos 46239/40/45 were 'bumped' to lesser duties at Willesden, taking over express fitted freights to the north or some Wolverhampton turns. No 46245 *City of London* was here rostered to Wolverhampton and is seen at New Street on its return working to Euston. *Jim Hardy*

Above:
New Street was a classic station for contrast of sunlight and shade, its changing mood being the basis for many magical photographs taken by many well-known photographers over the years. Standard Class 5 4-6-0 No 73068 was westward bound and awaiting departure when seen here half sunlit and half in shade. The new New Street, now a wire tunnel beneath a canopy of concrete, can claim little of the charm of yesteryear, when steam hung high overhead and sunlight played among the girders. When steam traction reigned, when side-rods clanked and wheels were regularly 'tapped' in the station, scenes such as this were played out many times a day.
Jim Hardy

Above:
The complexity of lines in the area and their associated traffic were serviced by locomotive depots at Saltley, Aston and Monument Lane. Saltley was the largest and most important of the London Midland locomotive facilities, housing 177 locomotives in 1933, 180 in 1950 and 67 in March 1965. Opened in 1855, the depot became code 3 of the Midland Railway, and 21A in more recent years. It closed to steam on 6 March 1967. This area of the Saltley roundhouse was being used for the retubing of two Class 5 4-6-0s, Nos 45297 and 45065, when photographed towards the end of steam operations at the depot. *Brian Robbins*

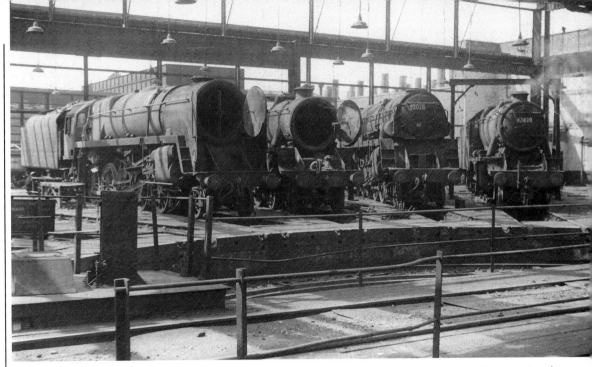

Above:
'9F' 2-10-0s and Stanier 2-8-0s are caught congregated round the Saltley turntable, with only the 2-8-0 (right) in light steam. The other locomotives were under servicing or light repair. Grime in plenty here, with ex-Crosti boilered

No 92028 without numberplate, but running with a none-too-well executed hand-painted version. On the other hand No 48628 retained its dignity with its official cast number plate still intact.
Brian Robbins

Above:
The Ivatt '2MT' 2-6-0s were highly competent and efficient machines, as were their tank engine counterparts. The 47ton locomotives were ideal for lighter duties, including this transfer freight made up of container flats which is seen passing the extensive Saltley Gasworks complex. A slight

modification was made to the later engines in the class in that the cylinder bores were enlarged by half an inch to 16½ in with the same 24in stroke. Note the arrow on No 46505's first conflat container; was this an embryonic BR logo?
Brian Robbins

Above:
A Peckett 'R1' 0-4-0ST (917/1902) was purchased by Albright & Wilson from the manufacturer in 1930 after it had been accepted back by Peckett on the sale of a new locomotive to its former owner, Crawshaw & Warburton of Shawcross in Yorkshire. It operated at the company's chemical works at Oldbury to shunt tanker wagons until withdrawn in August 1978. It was then preserved on the Chasewater Light Railway. *Mike Wood*

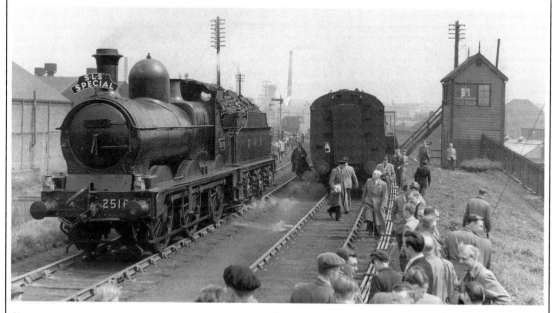

Above:
At the end of a long working life, 'Dean Goods' 0-6-0 No 2516 was the centre of attraction at Oldbury Town as SLS members and their guests detrained from a special that was touring Midland lines. The type was selected for over-seas service during World War 1, being extensively used by the Railway Operating Department. Strongly built, their 49ton weight ensured reasonable axle loadings for operation on lightly built lines at ROD facilities. Fortunately, on this May day in 1955, the wind was blowing the gaseous fumes from the chemical works away from the gathered assembly photographing and admiring this veteran near the signalbox. *Geoff Bannister*

Above:
W. G. Bagnall 0-4-0ST *J. T. Daly* (2450/1931) worked at the Horseley Bridge and Thomas Piggott's Great Bridge Works. The owners were engaged in the civil engineering business and the works survived into the 1990s (although rail traffic ceased in 1982). The locomotive departed for preservation at the Foxfield Railway on 19 July 1969 and is now on Alderney in the Channel Islands. The locomotive is seen on 4 January 1969. *Mike Wood*

Right:
Dudley in the late 1940s was served by two or three-coach autotrains from Walsall, hauled by veteran Webb 2-4-2Ts. The interchange station at Dudley Port witnessed intense activity below, as the Walsall-Dudley service was augmented by the 'Dudley Dasher', again push-pull 2-4-2T hauled, which plied back and forth between Dudley and Port some 20 times a day, connecting with main line services calling at the station above. Ryecroft (3C) had a small fleet of 2-4-2Ts for the service, and here the shed's No 46757 is being cleaned and serviced for another day's duties. It was photographed under Ryecroft's soon-to-be-demolished north-light roof. *Jack Haddock Collection*

Above:
Andrew Barclay 0-6-0ST *Peter* (782/1894) was unfortunately in derelict condition when the Pensnett Fuel Concentration Depot of Lund, Comley & Pitt Ltd was visited on 12 April

1969. *Peter* is now preserved at the Ironbridge Gorge Museum, where its condition has deteriorated still further. *Mike Wood*

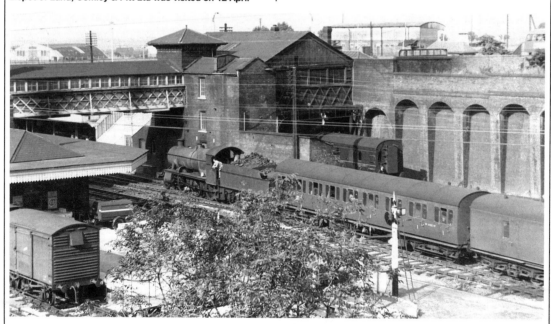

Above:
An unidentified '43xx' 2-6-0 had its face resolutely set towards Birmingham when seen on a visit to Dudley. Always an interesting station, Dudley was also served by the distinctive and successful early GWR AEC-built single-unit streamlined diesel railcars on local passenger services.

Proceedings at the architecturally-interesting Dudley Town station were visible from a high vantage point, which offered a different photographic perspective — perhaps more interesting than photographs from the more usual platform level.

Above:
The fireman of Johnson '2F' No 58261 looked somewhat dejected, either entranced by the whispy steam below or perhaps contemplating the heavy hammer work needed on the massive coal lumps in the tender. On 16 April 1955 there was no traffic offered for the 1.50pm Halesowen-Longbridge freight, at least in one direction. The Midland veteran is seen leaving Dowery Dell viaduct. With such an evocative name, who can deny the fanciful existence of Black Country fairies? After all, pigs were hung as pictures to decorate Black Country walls. *Geoff Bannister*

Above:
Windsor Street Gasworks was accessed from the now-lifted Aston goods branch. A Peckett (2058/1944) running solo gives us a more expansive view of the track at the site, with a fellow 'Greenhythe' (1812/1930) visible in the distance at the head of its train. Windsor Street works was closed on 23 February 1974, but was retained on stand-by basis in case it was required again. No 1812 met its end in the company of its workmate No 2058 at Cashmores of Great Bridge. *Mike Wood*

Above:
Round Oak Steelworks enjoyed royal patronage on a regular basis; 0-4-0ST *George VI* is pictured busy hauling one of the large cauldron wagons employed to haul slag and waste from the furnaces for disposal throughout the system. Note the wagon was fully coil sprung and carried on decorative holed wheel centres. The locomotive's shunter looked back on sister engine (or should it be daughter?) *Princess Margaret* seen raising steam in readiness for further duty.
Geoff Bannister

Above:
The British Sugar Corp's Foley Park factory at Kidderminster was situated on the west side of the town. Access to the works was from the southern end of the Severn Valley line. During the beet season two locomotives were normally in use daily. Andrew Barclay 0-4-0ST No 1 (1843/1925) was the only one of the three locomotives at the site not to survive into preservation. It is seen here on 15 March 1969.
Mike Wood

Right:
Andrew Barclay 0-4-0ST *Sir Thomas Royden* **(2088/1940)** trundled coal trucks for CEGB Stourport from the British Rail exchange sidings served by a short spur off the former GWR Kidderminster-Worcester line. The Stourport power station sidings terminated on a raised level gantry which accommodated loading chutes, mechanical wagon tipplers, offices and the locomotive depot. *Mike Wood*

Right:
This interesting cast-iron registration plate was affixed to the cab of a Peckett 0-4-0ST (1893/1936) when photographed at CEGB Stourport on 17 April 1970. The locomotive was delivered new to the West Midlands Joint Electricity Authority at Ironbridge in April 1936. GWR terms of registration for working over the company's lines included annual inspection of locomotives by the GWR locomotive inspector and examination of crews on operational procedure. *Mike Wood*

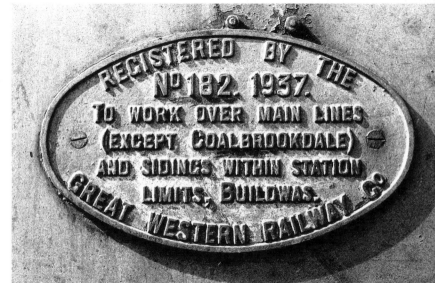

Right:
Hams Hall power station No 9 was a typically robust RSH 0-6-0T (3121/1944). No 9 was supplied to a City of Birmingham Electricity Services order and spent the whole of its working life at Hams Hall, where it was photographed outside the locomotive depot. *Mike Wood*

Above:
Young spotters welcomed prototype 'County' No 1000 *County of Middlesex* as it emerged from Wolverhampton tunnel at the head of train '1MO2'. The train would pass by the South signalbox under Sun Street bridge before coming to its Low Level platform stop. The LMS line from High Level to Heath Town and Bescot passed over the bridge in the background and in front of the steel-holding facility (top left).

Above:
In this superb panoramic view of Low Level, a 'King' awaits the right away with train 'A91'. Behind it, in the bay platform, a white plume of steam confirms the presence of a '64xx' 0-6-0PT with a single coach autotrain service to Dudley and Old Hill. Underneath the dominating skyline of Butler's Springfield Brewery (right) can be seen the covered accommodation of the carriage sheds, where a '94xx' 0-6-0PT and a '5101' 2-6-2T wait on pilot duties. On the skyline to the left of the photograph Stafford Road Works and its tall chimney stand clear above the retaining walls of the lines entering High Level (off picture left). South signalbox imposed its authority edging in from the right.
Simon Dewey

Wolverhampton

At Wolverhampton, the GWR was in conflict with the LNWR, but an added complication was that the GWR was also in conflict with itself! With broad gauge from the south to the town, the line to Shrewsbury was laid to 4ft 8½in. The government of the day accepted the report of a Board of Inquiry which favoured the latter as the norm, and the 'Battle of the Broad Gauge' was won, and lost, on Oxley viaduct. The Western, last to enter Wolverhampton, soon developed an extensive infrastructure which dominated the town. Low Level was not far from the town centre and extensive carriage sidings and Stafford Road MPD were but a half-mile away. On the other side of Stafford Road, the 'Factory' (Stafford Road Locomotive Works) was built, with Oxley freight yard and its large associated locomotive shed being a further half-mile to the north.

The rival High Level station, however, was closer to the town centre, just, and occupied a dominating position which overlooked the parallel GWR located only 30yd away to the east and 30ft below. The North Western locomotive shed was at Bushbury, a mile away, which was accessed by crossing the 22-arch Stour Valley viaduct. This viaduct spanned low ground drained by the Smestow Brook and also crossed the Birmingham Canal. The two companies were locked in direct competition for the lucrative London traffic, both concerns tapping the potential passenger and freight traffic of Britain's second city before going their separate ways towards the capital.

Below:
Express services from Wolverhampton to Paddington were either hauled in as empty stock from the carriage sidings at Cannock Road or came in from the north (Birkenhead or Shrewsbury). The latter trains were normally strengthened with additional coaches on arrival. Long devoid of its high overall roof, the station's up and down platforms had centre relief roads situated between them. These were used to house temporarily relieving locomotives. A local service is seen leaving the up bay as No 5059 *Earl St Aldwyn* awaited the road and its controlling signal with an afternoon Paddington express.

The 1923 Grouping made little difference to the status quo except that the GWR's opposition now had a new name — the London Midland & Scottish Railway. A few minutes knocked off the scheduled times of one company's expresses was soon matched by the other, neither side being allowed any continuing advantage. Stability was eventually achieved with honour, with both railways offering London-Birmingham times of 120min — the famous 'Two-Hour' expresses.

The travelling public was wooed by naming the principal services on each route; the Western named its train the 'Inter City'. Its rival, committed to serving the important towns of Coventry and Rugby, chose a more general and all-embracing title — the 'Midlander'. The Western's heritage of superb 4-6-0s served the line well up till 1962 and steam's withdrawal; its 'Saints', 'Stars', 'Castles' and 'Kings' overshadowing, but never eclipsing, the 'Georges' and

'Compounds' of the LMS. The LMS responded with its own 4-6-0s — the 'Patriots', 'Jubilees' and 'Royal Scots' — culminating with a flourish of Willesden 'Duchess' Pacifics on certain trains.

Perhaps the Stanier Pacifics could be considered to be the ultimate development of the Swindon line of locomotive development. No doubt eyes were raised in 1956 when the fabled 'Kings' were temporarily withdrawn from service due to bogie fracture problems. Although much of the rivalry was quelled by Nationalisation, old traditions died hard, and no doubt a few wise cracks greeted the fact that replacement power had been sought from 'the Midland'. No 46207 *Princess Arthur of Connaught* was one of the locomotives loaned. The Pacific looked massive when loading up at the Stafford Road coaler. Green became maroon, if only for a little while, and it did very well even if it lacked a copper-capped chimney.

Above:
Much of Wolverhampton's LMR traffic was diverted through Low Level as electrification work went ahead. The up 'Pines Express', for example, using WR lines from Wolverhampton and with WR motive power substituted. The 'Pines' headboard was carried for only a very short time, and photographs of the rerouted train showing this feature are rare. Unfortunately, details of Old Oak Common's single-chimneyed 'Castle' were obliterated by escaping steam, but there was no doubt about the train's reporting number below the headboard. Also interesting was the triple dummy signal for shunting. *Jim Hardy*

Right:
No 92221, with double chimney, has just traversed the goods avoiding lines to the east of Low Level, its load of wagons and 'Palvans' of perishables threading under Sun Street bridge. The buildings partly hidden by the locomotive's exhaust housed the GWR's motorised services for parcels and part-load distribution throughout the town and the northwest Midlands.

Centre right:
The clerestoried architecture of Butler's Springfield Brewery over-looked the Western; its clock indicating that it is 4.15pm as 'Grange' class 4-6-0 No 6871 *Bourton Grange* (84B) brought in empty stock from Cannock Road for a service to Oxford. Diverging left were the tracks of the 'New Engineers Siding' with the area inspection saloon seen housed under cover. The siding beyond the locomotive's front buffer beam often stabled vans of hops and malt, and was known as 'the Rhubarb' — the spillage was collected as a fertilizer which guaranteed to encourage rhubarb growth to 'show' standard; excellent for desserts and home-made wine.

Below right:
After receiving details of the make-up and weight of the stock — details irrelevant to a 'King' — from the guard, the crew prepared to haul the 'King Commemorative' rail tour from Cannock Road sidings uphill to Low Level to commence a trip to No 6000's birth-place. On arrival back at Wolverhampton after dark, the 'King's' footplate was full, with Foreman/Inspector Hughes hardly able to get aboard. In a terrific uphill start on curving track, the 'King' refused to slip as sparks blasted skywards, like a volcano, to a deafening exhaust. Then the regulator was eased for the down-hill straight to the carriage sidings. No 6000 provided us with a mar-vellous day, and a footplate experience the author will always remember.

Above left:
With electrification completed, Wolverhampton came under LMR operational control on 1 January 1963. WR locomotives were steadily phased out, being replaced by '5MTs', '8Fs' and various BR Standards. Bushbury and Stafford Road were closed, leaving Oxley as the centre of locomotive operations. Standard 5 No 73024 typified the change; it is pictured ready to depart from Low Level for Shrewsbury with a limited formation semi-fast. *Jim Hardy*

Left:
No 7024 *Powis Castle*, in 'Oxley' livery, is caught on the centre road awaiting an incoming train from the north. The author seldom took photographs from the inclined 'arcade', a long covered passage which linked Low Level with the LMR station above. With 'Castle' workings getting to be a rarity it was decided to take the plunge.

Above:
A solitary brake van was visible on 'the Rhubarb' beneath the Wednesfield Road bridge as the crew of ex-works Class 5 4-6-0 No 44681 was engaged in a tender-top dialogue — including a few well-chosen words — when discussing the work involved in getting the large coal lumps forward on the run north. Perhaps another tender dialogue was being exchanged at the platform end?

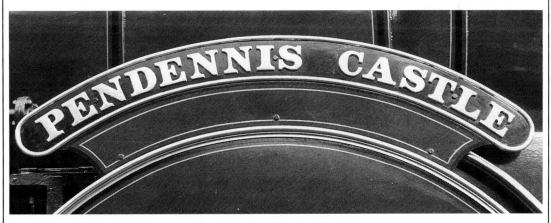

The traditional GWR nameplate as seen on No 4079 *Pendennis Castle*. *Mike Wood*.

In 1965 the north end of Low Level still witnessed steam haulage, but the writing was on the wall. The 'Cambrian Coast Express', brought in by the Class 47, was still entrusted to a BR Standard 4MT 4-6-0 for its journey to the coast via the Shrewsbury avoiding line. Main line diesel power predominated, with the incoming Class 47 (left) and a Class 40 awaiting a parcels working (below), whilst a Class 08 shunter was on pilot duties in the bay. The Wednesfield Road bridge neatly framed the available motive power on the ex-GWR main line to the north. This line was soon to be truncated and closed for through Paddington-Birkenhead services. Formerly a 'Castle' working, and finally worked by a 'King', the down 'CCE' without headboard and with Class 4MT haulage was but a shadow of the train's glory days prior to the decline of the Western. *Brian Robbins (both)*

Stafford Road and Oxley MPD's (84A & 84B)

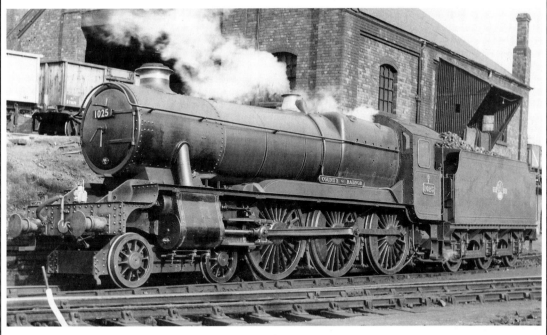

Above:
Wolverhampton's passenger locomotive facility was at Stafford Road (coded 'SRD' by the GWR and latterly 84A under BR). Intensive main line and local passenger services ensured constant activity at the turntable and coaling facility; locomotives were often turned and serviced for tight return schedules. No 1025 *County of Radnor* — strangely of 84G (Kidderminster) — received brickettes from the man-handled tipping skips. The tracks seen above the 'County' allowed coal to be gravity-fed to the skips from coal wagons shunted into position.

Below:
Ex-works locomotives from Stafford Road's 'Factory' normally powered the coal shunt. No 7413's light task would run-in new bearings and springs — no great steam output being required for the duty. The routine was simple, noisy and spectacular. Enter one Pannier, steam, smoke and clamour everywhere as it rushed the hill; cut off steam and hook up empties. A few accelerating exhausts, then coast down the hill. With the platform cleared of empties, an even noisier charge was made with four or five loads. Hook off, coast back to Stafford Road with the momentum gained down the steep incline. End of Duty.

Left:
Running Foreman Hughes was persuaded to line up with a driver for a photograph aboard an ex-works No 1472, which was temporarily stabled in the roundhouse. There were formerly three round-houses at 'SRD', but two were abandoned in the 1940s. After some light running-in, followed by any adjustments necessary, the 0-4-2T would be returned to its home depot to be put back into service.

Left:
Stafford Road was formerly the GWR's broad gauge depot in the town dating back to the 1850s. The broad gauge was abandoned in Wolverhampton in 1869 and throughout the GWR by 1892. No 7001 *Viscount Portal*, No 5026 *Criccieth Castle* and No 7006 *Lydford Castle* are shown being prepared for duty in what was once the broad gauge tender shop. It later became the main four-road straight running shed. Note the fire-irons leant against the cab of No 7006 and yet another load of accumulated smokebox and firebox ash being tipped from the barrow. *Hugh Ballantyne*

Left:
The shed yard at 84A was pho-tographed when cleaning stan-dards were being allowed to slip on the run-down to closure. From the introduction of the winter timetable in 1962 the 'Paddingtons' were diesel-hauled. Only one 'King', No 6019, was allo-cated new to Wolverhampton, but the shed's average of four or five was increased to 11 following the dieselisation of West of England routes. Stafford Road Works, tall chimney still denoted activity, while to the right Dunstall Park station and signalbox can just be seen over the wall. Sadly, the 'Kings' and 'Castles' in store would see no further service. The taper 0-6-0PT was No 9435 (84A).

Above:
An anorak-clad youngster, no doubt using an Ian Allan 'abc', noted the passing of an up freight through Dunstall Park. Controlling signals clearly outlined the track north past Stafford Road Works (left) to Oxley viaduct, visible centre right. No 6861 *Crynant Grange* was about to pass under the ex-LMS Stour Valley line on its Oxley-Banbury yard working.

Below:
Stafford Road in better times, with the yard graced by the classic lines of a 'King' cleaned and waiting for the 'off'. The platforms of Dunstall Park station overlooked the often pungent gasworks. East wind or west, the passengers at Dunstall Park could not win; if from the west you could at least see what was causing the offence and take its number! No 6005 *King George II* is seen, although its actual allocation cannot be determined from the photograph; the final 'Kings' were all withdrawn in 1962.

Above:
'King' class No 6021 *King Richard II*, its tender well emptied from its down journey, still had steam to spare as it was turned on the 84A turntable. Wagons of locomotive coal and empties can be seen on the coaler's southern decking. The western face of the coaler, superbly lit by the afternoon sun, was photographically ideal and in constant use. The eastern face seldom saw duty except in an emergency or at times of high workload. Part of the extensive carriage sidings at Cannock Road can be seen to the right.

Below:
Old Oak Common's No 6024 *King Edward I* is pictured turned and awaiting coaling. The locomotive is proudly displaying the second version of the 'Inter-City' headboard, which featured the coats of arms of Wolverhampton, Birmingham and London. The rival 'Midlander' ran up to Euston, returning in the afternoon. Train 'AO5', the 'Inter-City', worked north from Paddington in the morning, returning in the afternoon. The 'Cornishman', the 9am Wolverhampton-Penzance service, was truncated to start from Birmingham in 1962 after working from Wolverhampton for 10 years.

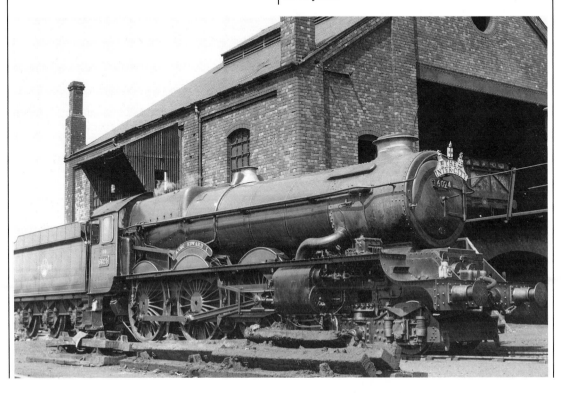

Above:
The repair work of a major steam locomotive depot was heavy and varied, the facility being capable of all types of heavy repair and servicing short of major overhaul or rebuilding, both of which were entrusted to the main works. Stafford Road's *King James I*, already displaying the 'A91' headboard for its next duty, was photographed being cleaned by the young enginemen of the future, whilst simultaneously receiving the attention of two fitters at work on the valve control rocker-arm linkage. 'Castle' No 7019 *Fowey Castle*, similarly in light steam, would continue to work in its accumulated grime. *Simon Dewey*

Right:
King Edward V, stationary near the coaling stage, was undergoing a 'blow down' procedure to eliminate accumulated scum and hard water insolubles from the water/steam interface near the top of the boiler. A build-up of impurities could induce the boiler to 'prime' with a possibility of serious water intake into the cylinders. The 'blow down' uses boiler steam to eliminate water and force the impurities to track level. It was often a noisy and spectacular display. *Simon Dewey*

Above:
The home of Wolverhampton's heavy freight power was Oxley (84B), a few hundred yards beyond Stafford Road and over Oxley viaduct. The shed also housed the useful 0-6-0PTs used for shunting, trip work and local passenger services. Oxley was based around two roundhouses with a double-sided coaling stage similar to that at Stafford Road. Photography was never easy inside the roundhouses, but No 9640 was nicely positioned on the turntable in round-house No 1. The locomotive, albeit devoid of number plates, was simmering steadily as it awaited allocation to one of the radiating storage roads. *Brian Robbins*

Below:
The pugnacious little Pannier tanks lined up on the left make a striking contrast with the Stanier Class 5 and Standard Class 9F beyond. Extensive smoke extraction hoods helped to reduce smoke levels inside the shed. A fine sunny day provided enough light for reasonable photography. On a day of rain or gloom you could either use flash or not bother. *Brian Robbins*

Above:
A Sunday afternoon visit to Oxley could often turn up a '47xx' heavy express freight 2-8-0 in a reasonable position in the yard. In the summer this class had the opportunity to demonstrate its flexibility, often hauling relief passenger services from Paddington to holiday destinations in the west. No 4700, in lined green livery alongside a 'Grange', provided the opportunity for a side-three-quarters view. The '47xx' class of nine locomotives was built between 1919 and 1923; the last was withdrawn in 1964.

Below:
'43xx' class 2-6-0 No 6388 clearly heralds its elevation to Class 1 duty by the '1A70' chalk adornment on the smokebox door. With the closure of 84A in 1963, Stafford Road's allocation of locomotives in good condition was transferred to Oxley; the others were withdrawn and scrapped. The external condition of double-chimneyed 'Castle' No 7024 *Powis Castle* probably cloaked the potential of a locomotive still in good mechanical condition. *Jim Hardy*

Above:
Stanier Class 5 No 44865 was photographed being loaded with coal at the west face of Oxley's coaling stage in February 1967. GWR coaling facilities were very labour intensive. They were also very dirty places, with constant clouds of coal dust swirling around as the four-wheeled skips were gravity fed from the coal wagons and then tipped into the insatiable tenders. The coaling stop was often used to clean the fire as the resulting ash heap showed. Twenty-four-hour operation was necessary, but the illumination, like the coaling facility, could be considered pretty basic, if not primitive. Any member of the coaling staff transferred from Bushbury would certainly have missed that shed's more modern facilities. Bushbury had both ash disposal and coaling towers. *Simon Dewey*

Above:
The remains of an almost non-existent tarpaulin weather sheet — high-tec stuff indeed — flapped in the breeze as a '2MT' 2-6-0, '3MT' 2-6-0 and Stanier '8F' lined up with the Dunstall Park racecourse grandstands seen in the background. The picture was taken through the southern portal of the Oxley coaler. *Simon Dewey*

Below:
Oxley seemed to be used as the secret development centre for the perfection of a heavy duty garden sprinkler, cunningly disguised as a locomotive watering column. The 'bag' had sprung a serious leak, its shower potential perhaps not being appreciated by the crew servicing No 44865. Crew obviously doubled up as fire cleaners and ash disposal teams judging by the huge residual ash pile which seemed about to take over the whole area around the water column. *Simon Dewey*

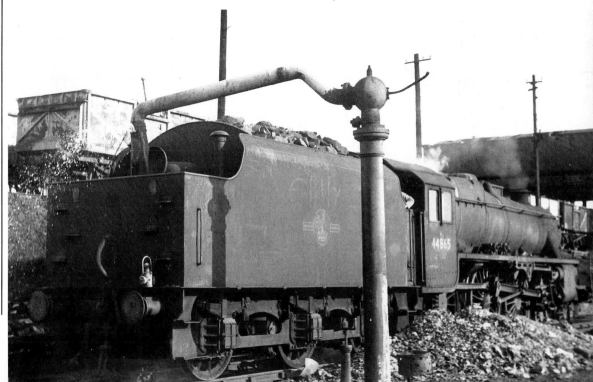

Above:
Two Stanier-designed locomotives flank consecutively-numbered ex-Crosti 2-10-0s in the roundhouse. The Brighton-designed '9Fs' appeared in 1954, with the 10 Crosti-boilered variants the following year. The complex pre-heat double-barrel boilers offered little or no advantage and locomotives so fitted were quickly returned to as near standard form that expense would allow short of total reboilering. 1957 saw the introduction of double chimneys and in 1958 Nos 92165-7 were equipped with double chimneys and mechanical stokers. The class was fitted with five types of tender (BR1B/1C/1F/1G/1K), which all varied in coal and water capacity and weight. The '9Fs' had ridiculously short lives as steam rapidly succumbed to the all-conquering diesel and electric locomotives. Nos 44805, 92021 and 92022. *Brian Robbins*

Below:
A cab view of a stoker-fitted '9F' 2-10-0. Grouped right were the fireman's controls for directing the coal feed to various areas of the firebed. To the right of the right-hand water gauge the slightly-angled dials allowed the driver to be informed of boiler status. Under the open butterfly firedoors can be seen the inclined plane of the screw feed from tender to firebox.

Right:
The stored locomotives at the north end of Oxley were perfectly framed by the spectacle plate of an Ivatt '2MT' 2-6-0. *Simon Dewey*

Below:
'Patriot' No 45531 *Sir Frederick Harrison*, **based at Crewe, brought a freight from its home town to Oxley on Friday and stayed the weekend, returning north on the Monday. No 45531 was but a stone's throw from its previous home at Bushbury; the rebuild previously being a star performer on the Wolverhampton-Euston expresses. The glory days were over and '31' fitted in well with the usual Oxley colour scheme of all-over grime.** *Brian Robbins*

Around Wolverhampton

Top:
Unlike Low Level, the LMR station at Wolverhampton retained its overall roof. High Level had three main platform faces, with bays at each end of the station and goods avoiding lines to the east. 'Royal Scot' No 46126 *Royal Army Service Corps* of Willesden was on the returning 'Birmingham Scotsman' duty when accompanied by Met-Cam and Birmingham RC&W diesel units on terminating local services. It is unbelievable that today's valuation of a 'Scot's' nameplate and crest is higher than the total asking price of the locomotive and tender on withdrawal from service. The station was radically altered on the electrification of the route.

Above:
Sand was being applied to the rails as No 46126 left on the final leg of its run to Birmingham. The section was always speed restricted in addition to the usual pw slacks for track repair, but this would cause few problems to the highly competent 'Scot'.

Above:
The regimental names of the 'Royal Scots' were well-suited to their no-nonsense competence and capabilities. One of the shortest names ever carried was that on No 6121; in fact, it was not even a name but the letters 'H.L.I.'. Later the name was revised and perhaps went overboard in the other direction becoming *Highland Light Infantry, City of Glasgow Regiment*. No 46115 *Scots Guardsman*, however, had a single-row nameplate, its simple letter-type contrasting strongly with the GW's 'Egyptian'-style.
No 46115 was built in September 1927 and rebuilt in August 1947 with a 2A taper boiler. The locomotive was the last of the class — in December 1965 — to be withdrawn.

Centre right:
City of London eased its returning Euston service over the curves past Millers flour mill and No 2 signalbox on leaving High Level. The trackbed was built on a high embankment past Bailey Street and passed over several main arterial roads leaving Wolverhampton after the crossing of Crane Street Junction. The power and speed of No 46245 would be better used south of Birmingham. *Jim Hardy*

Right:
LMR freight was handled at Wednesfield Road goods terminal, close to High Level. The moderately-sized yard was traditionally shunted by a Bushbury 'Super D' 0-8-0 — on this occasion No 48895. Principally a steel distribution yard, the office work and train despatch orders were originated in the substantial little office, its alternating brick courses being in 'headers' and 'stretchers'. *Jim Hardy*

Above:
Stanier 2-6-4T No 42659, in ex-works condition, graced the holding sidings east of High Level after a running-in turn, light engine from Crewe Works. A few of these excellent locomotives were based at Ryecroft for the more important and heavier local duties, and were very popular with 3C crews. The lighter '3P' Fowler parallel boiler 2-6-2Ts were sluggish performers and poor steamers. Generally disliked, they were usually limited to three coaches on the Birmingham-Rugeley turns over Cannock Chase.

Below:
'Jinty' 0-6-0T No 47437 returned to its Bushbury home in a noisy and smoky manner after banking a substantial '76xxx'-hauled freight up to Wolverhampton. The crew aboard was possibly contemplating the easier life to come represented by the newly-erected electrification supports north of the station. However, the new creature comforts would be available elsewhere as Bushbury was to close in 1965 and its allocation transferred to Oxley. *Brian Robbins*

Above:
Bushbury's No 45405 blackened the sky as it pounded over the Stour Valley viaduct with a heavy mixed freight for Wolverhampton. The fireman, up for a breather, ensured that Stafford Road depot below could not miss the passing of one of the highly-successful 4-6-0s designed by an ex-Swindon man.

Bushbury veterans Nos 58295 and 58128 were available for Sunday afternoon photography backed by an array of '4F', '8F' and Class 5 shedmates at Bushbury. The Midland '2Fs' were useful power for shunting and transfer freight duties around Wolverhampton and Walsall.

Shadows of 1956 and Stanier Pacifics covering 'King' diagrams. The penultimate Stanier Pacific, No 46256 with modified rear-end frame and cab, was a rare visitor to 84A after working a pigeon fanciers' special into Wolverhampton — reporting code 3K23 — on 22 June 1963. 'Coo' was probably the correct evocation on seeing '56' awaiting its return journey; 'how are the mighty fallen'. *Simon Dewey*

Stafford Road Works was officially closed on 1 June 1964. Part of the facility had been built on the location of the original Shrewsbury & Birmingham Railway's terminus at Wolverhampton (built in 1849), which was demolished when the more central High Level, then Queen Street, was built. Churchward-designed heavy freight 2-8-0 No 3807, with later side-windowed cab, was under repair when the 'Factory' was visited by Simon Dewey. Note the heavy duty traversing crane at the far end of the erecting hall. *Simon Dewey*

Top:
Stafford Road Works in 1956. With the demise of steam operations, the 'Factory' was to close in 1964. What appears to be a 'Dean Goods' in backwards view (left) was, in fact, a separate tender under repair standing behind a dismantled 0-6-0PT (either No 3608 or 4608). *Geoff Bannister*

Above:
A visit to Courtauld's Wolverhampton complex proved interesting on 31 December 1957 with the company's Peckett 0-4-0ST *Daffyd* putting in a spell of duty in the industrial heartland of England — a considerable distance from its normal duties at Flint. Motive power was obviously a problem as the diminutive ex-L&YR Aspinall Class 21 0-4-0ST No 51204 was also on loan during November and December 1957. *Geoff Bannister*

Above:
Regional meeting at Wolverhampton; ex-GWR tracks, ex-LMS Class 5 with Southern headcode discs and Eastern stock! No 44691 had eased below Cannock Road bridge to approach the carriage sidings to dispose of the stock from a Portsmouth-Wolverhampton summer Saturdays working. A locally-built Guy double-deck bus neared its Wolverhampton birthplace on a service from Cannock. *Simon Dewey*

Below:
'G2A' No 49070 trundled steadily past Littles Lane and Wolverhampton No 4 signalbox north of High Level with an assorted local freight in 1962. *Simon Dewey*

Above:
Oxley branch meeting! 'Grange' class No 6800 *Arlington Grange* was photographed coming off the Oxley branch as it eased past No 6925 *Hackness Hall*, which was awaiting clearance on a westbound freight for Stourbridge Junction in September 1963. *Simon Dewey*

Below:
Stanier '8F' No 48740, in superb condition, was opened up as the Oxley home signal dropped. The train was a Stanlow-Albion Gulf oil train. The van acted as a barrier wagon. The cabside star indicated that the '8F' was fully balanced for express freight duties.

Above:
An unidentified '9F' 2-10-0 with a block Stanlow-Albion Gulf tank train was pictured passing canal and ex-GWR lines by Stafford Road depot. The far arch gave access to the depot, its neighbour spanning the main ex-GWR running lines. The 84A coaler can be seen under the extreme left arch. The '9F' would still have to continue its steep climb on a high embankment before reaching the relative flat of High Level station goods lines. *Brian Robbins*

Below:
'9F' 2-10-0 No 92110, workstained but photogenic, was another locomotive engaged on Stanlow-Albion Gulf traffic photographed on the approach to Oxley yard. The tanks were recently new from works, not carrying, therefore, the oil-spillage and grime they would show after a few weeks in such service.

Above:
A '9F' approaching Oxley sidings is about to cross Oxley viaduct, which spanned the Birmingham Canal, with a mixed van train. Stafford Road Works, built in its dominant position and close to 84A and 84B, could accommodate the smaller locomotives for heavy repair, but other locomotives regularly seen at the 'Factory' included 'Halls', 'Granges', '28xx' 2-8-0s and 'Castles'. 'Kings' always went home to Swindon. The photograph was taken from the steep approach track to Oxley depot. *Brian Robbins*

Below:
A wintry world of frost, ice and snow predominated as an unidentified 'Grange' accelerated north from Oxley with a Banbury-Chester freight. Cold fingers just managed to function to produce this photograph, which made the long cold wait worth while.

Top left:
The Donnington Lane bridge in the background was situated midway between Cosford and Albrighton. It was the location of many of the author's earliest experiences in watching trains as Western freights headed downhill at near express speeds. By the time Brian Robbins recorded the passing of No 44963 at the head of a Birkenhead-Paddington service both the track and motive power were LM-owned — but at least the locomotive was still, thankfully, steam. *Brian Robbins*

Centre left:
Heavy Churchward 2-8-0 No 2802 powered through Codsall at speed in March 1954 with a substantial freight from Crewe Gresty Lane to Stoke Gifford via Wombourn. The canopies have long since disappeared from the surviving remains of this ex-Shrewsbury & Birmingham Railway station. *Geoff Bannister*

Bottom left:
'County' class 4-6-0 No 1016 *County of Hants* left a substantial trailing exhaust when speeding a Birkenhead-Paddington express through Codsall on 4 August 1956. The 'County' class maintained a steady West Midlands presence, being based at Chester and Shrewsbury. They were, however, designed with the severe gradients of the South Devon banks in mind. *Geoff Bannister*

Above right:
City of Truro, restored to main line running condition, was an obvious and popular choice of Great Western motive power for the SLS's journey from Wolverhampton to Swindon Works on 16 June 1957. The train is seen passing Monmore Green and approaching Priestfield Junction. The gantry had a splitting distant controlling entry to the Dudley (West Midland) line, formerly part of the old OW&W. *Geoff Bannister*

Below right:
The '2301' class 0-6-0s, introduced in 1883, were long-lived and versatile locomotives on both main and branch line duties, and were popular machines. No 2516 had put in many useful years of service before being selected as motive power for the SLS's 'West Midland' rail tour on 21 May 1955. The old 'Dean' replenished its water tank at Wombourn as the passengers detrained to record the veteran on film. *Geoff Bannister*

55

Above left:
A single bogie tank was the only traffic on offer for 0-6-0PT No 6422 on 26 April 1957, when it was rostered to cover the Saturdays Only Courtauld's siding-Oxley sidings train. It was photographed at Oxley Branch Junction. Tank traffic to Courtauld's factory mainly carried caustic soda.
Geoff Bannister

Below left:
Recently ex-works, '28xx' class 2-8-0 No 2850 undertook the local freight trip working from Oxley to Baggeridge Junction. It is seen approaching Oxley Branch Junction. The triangle formed by this junction along with Oxley North Junction and Oxley Middle Junction proved very useful for turning loco-motives if Stafford Road's turntable was unserviceable or under repair. *Geoff Bannister*

Above:
Ambling along south through a purple sea of rosebay willow-herb, No 44872 was not extended by the lightweight four-van Shrewsbury-Birmingham parcels train as it worked into a deep wooded cutting south of Albrighton. With a clear exhaust and steam to spare, the fireman was taking things easy, looking at the natural history and wildlife along the line as he admired the view.

Above:
There was little general activity at Wellington as two passengers waited on the down platform and 'Grange' class 4-6-0 No 6839 *Hewel Grange* lifted its long Oxley-bound freight train past the locomotive shed at Wellington. Several Panniers and Prairies were based at Wellington for local branch line freight and passenger duties.

Above right:
Perhaps there is no official collective noun for a grouping of ex-GWR 0-6-0PTs, but there was a 'plenitude of Panniers' at Wellington when Jim Hardy visited the station for a photographic session — Nos 9630, 3744, 9724 and 3776 enjoyed each other's company as they awaited further work. The handy little locomotives were to be found throughout the ex-GW system and their 'tackle anything' propensity has proved a valuable asset in service on preserved lines. *Jim Hardy*

Below right:
Using an American colloquialism 'meanwhile back at the ranch', in this case 'at the back of the shed', a forlorn Stanier 0-4-4T No 41900, drafted in for local train duties, stood with chimney 'bagged'. No 41900 was built as No 6400 in 1932 following Stanier's appointment as CME; it was the first of a class of 10. Perhaps the 'foreigner' to the Western men was too much to stomach, or perhaps it was even a 'below the belt' transfer from the Midland, but traditions die hard and the author never saw it work again. It was finally withdrawn in March 1962.

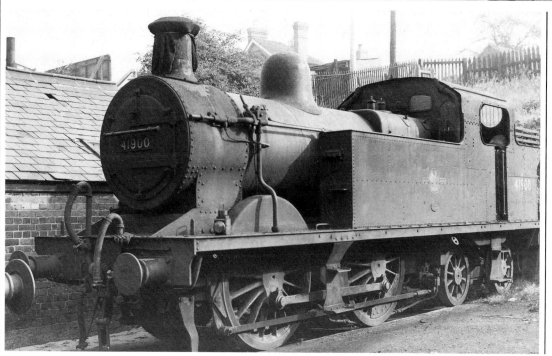

Top:
Stafford crews, however, appreciated the worth of the elegant Fowler 2-6-4Ts, strong and easy runners for the Salop locals passing through Wellington. Stafford (5C) made a point of keeping its small fleet of these locomotives — Nos 42309 and 42389 along with the 1933-built No 42400 (which differed in having a side-window cab) — immaculately clean. '09', built in February 1929, lifted its safety valves as it prepared to depart from its Wellington stop on a return working to Stafford. No 42309 was withdrawn in September 1964.

Above:
This delightful photograph epitomises the action on many evocative branch lines in the West Midlands. 2-6-2T No 4142 was running under easy steam at Farley Dingle (wonderful name!) on 23 April 1957 on a Much Wenlock-Wellington afternoon local service. As so often happens when rural railway services are withdrawn, the trackbed was transformed into part of the modern road system. *Geoff Bannister*

Right:
Stanier '8F' No 48220 was working hard at the head of a misty Coalbrookdale heading empties from Ironbridge power station to Kemberton colliery on 3 January 1967. The '8F' was photographed, during the final weeks of steam operation on the line, from the platform at Greenfield Halt. *Geoff Bannister*

Above:

Coalbrookdale Ironworks' 0-4-0ST No 5 was built in 1865 for use at the company's own works. It was later sold to the Netherseal Coal Co, Derbyshire, and then on to Ellis & Everard for service at the company's Bardon Hill quarry, Leicestershire. It returned to Coalbrookdale for preservation in October 1959 and was photographed at the Allied Ironfounders Museum, now part of the Ironbridge Gorge Museum Trust.

Below:

Peckett 'W6' 0-4-0ST No 1 (1803/1933) was parked near to the locomotive shed in the late afternoon sunshine, set in the pleasant surroundings of the Ironbridge Gorge and CEGB Ironbridge power station on 20 February 1971. No 1 was preserved on the Foxfield Railway when withdrawn from service. *Mike Wood*

Above:
The Much Wenlock & Severn Junction Railway was opened in 1862, its station at Buildwas Junction becoming overshadowed by the Ironbridge 'A' power station that opened in 1932. 0-6-0PT No 7744 was engaged on a Wellington-Much Wenlock afternoon service during April 1957. Beneath the water tank, the water column 'bag' was safely stowed beside the 'fire-devil' for winter warmth. 'A' station was demolished and replaced by the much later 'B' station, part of that development being over the old junction site. *Geoff Bannister*

Below:
When connections did connect; three trains and two platforms were recorded at Buildwas Junction on 29 April 1957. Western 0-6-0PTs Nos 5712 and 4614 continued to simmer gently as a GWR streamlined AEC diesel railcar was just visible through the open gate engaged on a Severn Valley duty. No 4614 was in charge of the Shrewsbury-Hartlebury service with No 5712 on the Much Wenlock-Wellington 'stopper'. Unbelievably, a fourth train, from Wellington to Wenlock, had worked through the station and had reversed behind No 5712 and so was out of sight of the camera. *Geoff Bannister*

Left:
White exhaust was lifted high over the cab as No 3732 was rostered to the daily freight from Much Wenlock to Longville on 25 September 1954. The 0-6-0PT passed luxuriant lineside vegetation and farmland as it continued on its energetic way through the rolling countryside near Stretton Westwood. *Geoff Bannister*

Below:
The Colonel **after its long working life at the Grove colliery and on Cannock Chase, was transferred to the Granville colliery near Wellington. The Hudswell Clarke-built locomotive, dating from 1914, was seen taking a brief break between shunting activity; the shunter is likewise 'taking five' as he leaned on a steel wagon of power station 'fines'. Giesl-fitted 'Austerity' Granville No 5 meanwhile took water at the servicing facility in front of the shed.** *Mike Wood*

Shrewsbury and West

Above:
The annual Talyllyn Railway special was a photographer's dream due to its unusual and interesting motive power. 'Dukedog' No 9017 was paired with a side-window '73xx' 2-6-0 as it was photographed passing the locomotive depot and approaching Sutton Bridge signalbox and junction in Shrewsbury. The train would diverge here to head towards the Cambrian line to continue its journey to Towyn.

Below:
'Manor' class 4-6-0 No 7819 *Hinton Manor*, cleaned and presentable as usual, started to move forward along the platform at Shrewsbury on being given the signal and green flag by the guard with the departing down 'Cambrian Coast Express'. The departure is watched by a group of young enthusiasts, notebooks at the ready. *Jim Hardy*

Below:
When the gleaming lined 'Manors' were replaced by BR
Standard Class 4MT 4-6-0s the 'CCE' did not seem to fit the
glamour of its name. Often with locomotives in a dirty condition and with the headboard absent, the impact of the passing express was diminished. No 75053 was photographed in
the mid-1960s as it crossed to the Cambrian line towards
Welshpool at Sutton Bridge Junction. However, even this
train had impact in comparison with the modern day equivalent — Class 158 DMUs.
Brian Robbins

Above right:
Steam blasted violently skywards from the safety valves of
'Britannia' Pacific No 70023 *Venus* as the locomotive was
eased over the pointwork north of Shrewsbury station to

take the Crewe line with '1M02'. The class was designed
with the simplicity of two-cylinder maintenance and servicing in mind. This train was the Saturdays Only Bournemouth
West-Manchester Piccadilly service — the 'Pines Express' —
which was steam worked from Wolverhampton Low Level to
Crewe by this date. *Jim Hardy*

Below right:
A job that could not be rushed: the ritual watering of locomotives would be witnessed at depots and platform ends
dozens of times a day throughout the whole railway system.
The driver of this Shrewsbury-based 0-6-0PT, his mate temporarily absent, used the moral and physical support of a
concrete post as the lengthy process was completed. With
Shrewsbury Abbey visible beyond the column and Sutton
Bridge signalbox behind the camera.

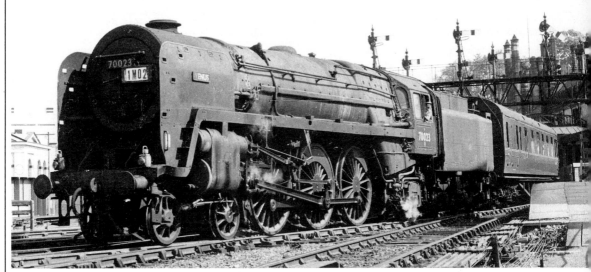

Sheeted wagons containing ammunition formed the train behind 1897-designed '2021' class 0-6-0PT No 2144 on the Cleobury Mortimer & Ditton Priors Light Railway. The locomotive was photographed passing Burwarton Halt on its journey to Ditton Priors on 23 February 1954. Trains on the branch ran three times a week to the Royal Navy Ammunition Depot. The spark-arresting chimney was a necessary feature for work on this particular line. *Geoff Bannister*

A well-cleaned No 2144 was admired by the gathered photographers as it paused at Cleobury North crossing on 21 May 1955. Spring was a little late that year and the elm trees are still devoid of their luxuriant green canopies. The delightful countryside traversed by this little line would have been appreciated by the SLS members and their guests travelling on the special train. *Geoff Bannister*

Below left:
An incoming Festiniog Railway Society special brought an immaculate Churchward heavy mixed traffic 2-8-0, No 4701 in lined green livery, to Shrewsbury. The portrait view gave a good impression of the size of these locomotives, with their 5ft 8in driving wheels. The locomotive weighed 82 tons — two tons more than a 'Castle'.

Above:
Another fascinating rural delight was the Clee Hill branch. 0-6-0PT No 9716 was engaged with shunting activity, its movement and single coal wagon being overseen from the small signalbox controlling Bitterley Yard. The rope-hauled 'runner-wagon' stood on the left at the base of the steep incline which served stone quarries some 600ft higher and a mile and a quarter distant. The total train weight allowed on the incline was 65 tons, hauled and braked from the higher level using a 1½in diameter steel cable. *Geoff Bannister*

Above:
This picture of Bescot depot, taken earlier than the next illustration, shows the Wellman Smith mechanical coaling plant erected in 1936 and also its associated ash disposal facility by M. B. Wild & Co. A wide assortment of motive power was lined up, as usual, on the Sabbath, including 'Jubilee' No 45648 *Wemyss*. The old Bescot station was still substantially present (top right) with new crewing facilities built in brick being erected on the shed side of the main line running tracks.

Below:
The 'Bescot Sunday Simmer' again, this time shown from a viewpoint a little further down the yard. This allows us to illustrate the huge water tank with running roads beneath it. The yard had been rationalised and electrified, having huge illumination pylons to aid shunting and train preparation throughout the 24hrs of each day. Nos 48726, 48556 and 44840 can be seen closest to the camera.

Walsall, Cannock and Cannock Chase

The area round Walsall was the centre of intense heavy industrial development as the town was situated on the edge of the Black Country coalfield. This coalfield was already in decline by the start of the 20th century. The area also had some ironstone deposits and a wealth of limestone. The latter was mined to the east of Walsall in what is now the town's Arboretum — an extensive wooded park containing a large lake. Unlimited limestone for flux was available at the Wren's Nest, Dudley, which is now a nature reserve but was formerly of great palaeontological significance as a result of the number and quality of its Silurian Age fossils. One large trilobite, Calymene blumenbachi, was known locally as the 'Dudley Locust'.

With coal, ironstone and limestone flux readily available, the Black Country to the west of Walsall became famous for its metal manufactories. Heavy development taxed the transport capability of the early roads and canals, and railways infiltrated the area. The arrival of the railways spurred further industrial development, goods being produced that were easily transported within the loading gauge.

Walsall's Ryecroft depot was not only the centre of passenger operations, but heavy freight power and shunters were also based there. Bescot, a couple of miles away, was the true home of the freight locomotive, however, as the principal depot in the area (coded 3A), with Bushbury (3B), Ryecroft (3C), Aston (3D) and Monument Lane (3E). Bescot, Bushbury and Walsall were always strong in North Western power, the dominant 0-8-0s eventually giving way to Stanier types before the end of steam operations. Walsall was the nodal point for the distribution of coal pouring in from the Cannock branch, the Cannock Chase coalfield developing to replace the Black Country field as the latter declined into oblivion.

Below:
Seen against the old Bescot station, demolished and replaced by an unglamorous 'bus shelter' on electrification of the line, 'G2A 'Super D' 0-8-0 No 49125 was turned on the Bescot turntable in readiness for its next duty.

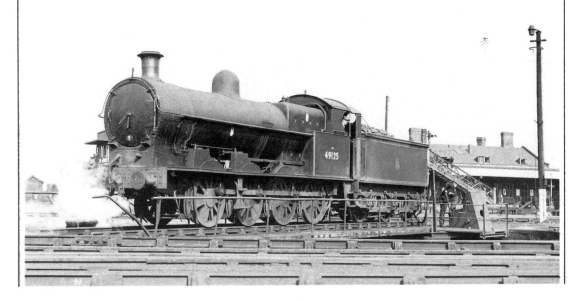

No 48767 in typical Stanier '8F' style made a footsure and spirited departure from Bescot yard with a substantial train load of coal. The rafts of HAAs were yet to come, the '8F's' load being a highly assorted mixture of both wood and steel mineral wagons, some of which were loaded with considerable-sized coal. Heading out towards Walsall the freight would probably swing left and up the incline to attain the level of the Dudley line, where its household and industrial fuel would be distributed throughout the Black Country.

No 58181 of Bescot was a Johnson ex-Midland 0-6-0 with 4ft 11in driving wheels. It was built in 1875, with the class being rebuilt from 1917 onwards when Belpaire boilers were incorporated. Reduced to lesser duties in old age, it is perhaps difficult to realise that the class was introduced as the heavy main line freight power of its day. The '2F' was allocated to shunting duties adjacent to the dominating BOAK building near to Walsall station.

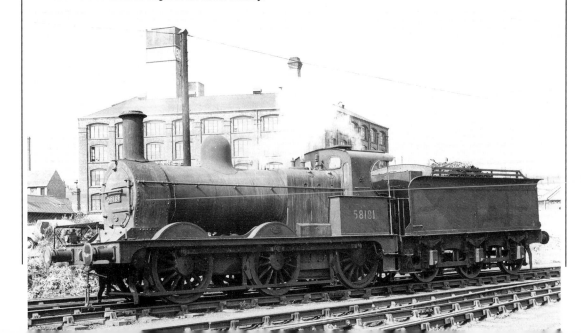

Above:
Nos 40646 and 40694 were retained at Bescot for use on the District Engineer's inspection saloon and were kept very clean for such work. The 4-4-0s, with 6ft 9in driving wheels, were also very useful for excursion and trip traffic during the summer months, backing up Bescot's top-line excursion locomotive No 44766, a double-chimney Stanier Class 5. No 40646 especially became very popular haulage for Bill Camwell's SLS specials which toured both highways and byways throughout the Midlands before the '2P's' final demise. Its twin No 40694 had just come on shed and stood between coaler and ash facility awaiting the disposal crew's attention. No 40694 was built in November 1932 and was withdrawn exactly 30 years later.

Below:
Another world! Five guard's vans and a jackshaft drive diesel-electric 0-6-0 shunter graced Bescot yard as Jack Haddock photographed an ex-works 'Scot' on the shed — an extremely rare event at Bescot. With no sign of steaming showing on the boiler of the immaculate No 46132, *The Kings Regiment Liverpool*, must have journeyed from Crewe to Bescot as a special hauled delivery in the consist of an incoming freight. With its regimental association No 46132 would perhaps have been better allocated to Edge Hill (Liverpool) for its main line duties, rather than 21A (Saltley). Note the regiment's crest above the nameplate.
Jack Haddock

Above:
Not all the best photographs were, or are, taken on very expensive equipment. An uncommon visitor to the Ryecroft turntable in 1954 was the prototype 'Patriot' No 45500, which was the LMS's memorial locomotive dedicated to those who lost their lives in World War 1. Jack Haddock's photograph was his first attempt, taken on a 116 'Box' camera. The fireman was attempting to stow the harpoon shaped 'dart' on the tender; such activity was to become highly dangerous under energised 25kV lines, where a proximity flashover might occur. To use fire-irons beneath the wires was STRICTLY forbidden. *Jack Haddock*

Below:
With electrification proceeding apace, Bescot's safety-conscious management undertook a training programme in readiness for live-wire running. A mock-up of an electrified section was made with wooden gallows complete with non-powered wiring at the correct height to force home the point about limited clearances. Nos 40646 and 40694 were running with their own tenders when this Sunday afternoon picture was taken beneath the wires, the pair sharing the road with two Johnson '2F' 0-6-0s. Before their withdrawal the pair exchanged tenders, a clean No 40646 running with a grubby coal-railed tender from its withdrawn stablemate.

The Stanier version of the '3P' 2-6-2T locomotives was somewhat better than the sluggish Fowlers. Nos 71-144 were built in 1935 but, in June 1937, No 87 was fitted with a 6A boiler with large firebox. A further three — Nos 83, 114 and 139 — were similarly fitted and an additional six (Nos 142/48/63/67/69 and 203) were fitted with boilers with larger barrels and superheater (boiler type 6B). As no more were converted it would appear that the way forward was better suited to a 2-6-4T design. One of the original series, No 40083, was photographed at Bescot.

'Super D' 0-8-0s were popular for SLS specials and several tours used the type either singly or in pairs over the years. No 48930 was photographed from the train as it rounded the sharply inclined curve to join the South Staffordshire line to Dudley. An '8F' was held at signals with a freight for the west and an early 0-6-0 diesel, distant forerunner of Class 08, joined in the activity on 2 June 1962. The 0-8-0 is on the Bescot curve. *David Bradbury*

Above:
Several Cannock Chase colliery locomotives used unusual flat wagons accommodating three tipping hoppers for coal interchange operations to road or canal. Slewing chains showed prominently as NCB wagon No 476 with its three similarly-numbered hoppers was being hauled behind 'Austerity' 0-6-0ST No 2. The train, from the Essington inter- change sidings on the Cannock branch, was taking empties to Hilton Main colliery and was photographed crossing the Bursnip Road at Essington. The unique Bursnip Road crossing signalbox was obscured by smoke, but the LNWR-type signal remained sentinel with Holly Bank colliery visible on the skyline. *Geoff Bannister*

Above:
The signalbox/look-out point dominated the Bursnip Road crossing. This photo, taken from the opposite side of the road, affords a better view of the box and associated building. When Hilton Main closed, the building was used as a British Legion headquarters. Eventually vacated, it fell into disrepair but has recently been tastefully restored to near original condition as a home, its new lantern signalbox overlooking a non-existent crossing with non-existent railway traffic. *Jim Hardy*

Right:
Hilton Main colliery, near Featherstone (Wolverhampton), used this ex-Barry Railway 0-6-0T which was photographed in March 1950. Ex-GWR No 785 was formerly Barry Railway No 53 and was built by Hudswell Clarke (352/1891). *Geoff Bannister*

Top:
After service at Walsall Wood colliery, *Tony* was transferred to Hawkins' Old Coppice colliery at Cheslyn Hay. In this c1950 photograph shunter E. Ridgeway, driver W. Westwood and weighbridge clerk H. Jervis line up by the chunky tank locomotive with the colliery visible in the background. *Tony* was built by Hawthorne Leslie in 1921 (works No 3460).
The late Harold Tooth/Author's Collection

Above:
Hawkins' coal output was collected by Walsall '2F' 0-6-0s from the sidings which ran parallel to the A5. Coal from the colliery gained access to the Cannock branch by a steep incline on passing over the Station Road level crossing overlooked by the old Great Wyrley & Cheslyn Hay station. No 58122 was about to depart for Bescot yard with a short train of assorted coal.

Above:

Within a mile of Old Coppice was Mid Cannock colliery. Due to diversions and line closure at Armitage, this weekend van train of perishables was diverted via the Cannock branch and was photographed passing Mid Cannock. No 45530 *Sir Frank Ree* had steam to spare for the continuous climb to Bloxwich. It would shortly pass the author's old junior school at Landywood, where he used to watch the trains from the school yard.

Right:

On 30 April 1957 *Hawkins* was in the paintshop at Cheslyn Hay. This little locomotive was built by Peckett (809/1900). An assortment of paint tins, brushes and rags adorned the front buffer beam. A smart engine would soon be ready to return to its duties.
Geoff Bannister

Top:
Hednesford station in 1913 with a substantial train of six-wheel coaches hauled by a Webb 2-4-2T. This delightful period piece shows considerable activity on the up platform for an afternoon train to Walsall and Birmingham headed by an immaculately-groomed, but unidentified, locomotive of the 4ft 6in drivered series. *Mrs T. B. Dudley's Collection*

Above:
Bescot's No 49125 impressively lifted a heavy coal train from West Cannock No 5 colliery up the steep hill into Hednesford yard. Hednesford was an important reception and distribu-tion centre for coal from several Chase collieries. Walsall Ryecroft always provided one, sometimes two, 'Ds' for day-long shunting operations and trips to 'Fives'. These were additional to several Bescot-Hednesford runs by other 'Ds' and Staniers throughout the day.

Right:
Bescot's immaculate Stanier Class 5 with double chimney, No 44766, was seldom seen at Hednesford, as it was kept for excursion work or long-distance fitted freights. The Stanier posed with its van in Hednesford yard while the duty 0-8-0 made up its train.

Cannock Chase

Cannock Chase can be likened, geologically, to a large, upside-down saucer; the higher, undulating plateau dropping down to the flatter lands and river valleys that surround it. Capped by massive thicknesses of Bunter Pebble beds and sands which are exploited in several quarries for concrete and building materials, the real wealth of the Chase was deep coal. This was formerly mined in several workable and productive seams. The anticlyne favoured economic railway operation, empties being taken up to the mines, whilst full loads were dropped down to the main line outlets giving access to countrywide distribution.

The industrial locomotives on Cannock Chase came from variously-owned colliery systems. The most important of these were Cannock & Rugeley (Rawnsley), Cannock Chase Colliery Co (Chasetown) and Littleton colliery (Huntington, Cannock). As collieries closed there was considerable locomotive transfer. The principal locomotive type was the highly-useful 0-6-0ST, with a few smaller 0-4-0STs from various manufacturers for lighter duties and pithead shunting. The Cannock Chase Colliery Co, however, had an early penchant for the 0-4-2ST; its fleet of Beyer-Peacocks going back to 1856. Their longevity was legendary, their short wheelbase was well-suited to the many tight curves on the system. *McClean* completed a century of service for the company, 1856-1956.

A unique Chase locomotive was the Rawnsley-based *Topham*, built by Bagnall of Stafford (2193/1922), which featured Walschaerts valve gear. However, the sound economics of the 'Austerity' 0-6-0ST could not be denied, with at least seven of the type being known to have worked on the Chase. Littleton alone used the services of four: No 2 (Hunslet 3772/1952); No 6 (RS&H 7292/1945); No 7 (HC 1752/1953); and No 8.

A feature of Chase operations was the smart turn-out of its locomotives. Deep bright blue with red frames and wheel centres was the general colour scheme, but West Cannock ran a green and a black Austerity. With many one-off or short-run designs running on the Chase from many manufacturers, there was plenty of variety. Photographic locations abounded, not only at pit heads, but also against wonderful coniferous and deciduous woodland, level crossings, scenic canal locations, cattle-filled pastures and farmsteads, particularly on the Littleton line. With hard-working locomotives, steeply-rising gradients and great scenery, the Chase was idyllic, annually graced by the Bentley and camera of the late Ivo Peters.

Alas the steam cacophony is no more, but, in November 1992, Littleton hosted the Foxfield 'Austerity' *Whiston* for the weekend; it was to be a weekend not without incident. An observant motorway traveller reported a Littleton diesel on fire. Soon the quiet lanes of Otherton witnessed blue flashing lights and sirens blaring as a full three-unit turn-out by the Staffordshire Fire Brigade sped to the rescue to find *Whiston* steaming away normally. The normality of Littleton 20 years ago had turned into a fiasco in the all-diesel age of 1992.

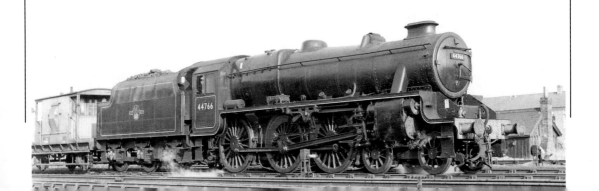

Above:
Hednesford's water column was kept busy throughout the day by heavy freight locomotives needing to top-up their tenders. Frost prevention was entrusted to the 'fire-devil' below the tank. The 0-8-0 was just pulling out of the yard with its heavy coal train bound for Walsall.

Above right:
Grove colliery at Little Wyrley, near Brownhills, was only a mile from the farm where the author grew up. Even nearer was the Great Wyrley No 3 colliery, from where billowed clouds of white steam and noise every time the pit cage ascended. Grove and Harrison's No 3 were joined by a narrow gauge rope-hauled surface line about ¾-mile in

length, where coal-filled 'tubs' and empties were hauled in strings like conkers. *The Colonel*, built by Hudswell Clarke in 1914, was photographed at Grove colliery on 30 April 1957. *Geoff Bannister*

Right:
The Cannock Chase Colliery Co purchased five 0-4-2STs from Beyer Peacock between 1856 and 1872. *McClean* (28/1856) did a century of service before being withdrawn in 1956. The company had an extensive railway network serving the 10 collieries it eventually owned. The photograph shows *McClean* coming off shed on 28 May 1926. The line was opened in February 1858 and closed in 1961.
The late Colling Turner/Mike Wood's Collection

Above:
Cannock and Rugeley colliery 'Austerity' 0-6-0ST No 3 (Hunslet 3789/1953) meandered down grade from Rawnsley past Bentley Brook with a load of power station 'fines' in September 1964. With reduced coal traffic from the colliery, Nos 3 and 8 were transferred to Granville colliery, Wellington, with the introduction of a Vulcan diesel at Rawnsley in 1966. This left the last 'Austerity', No 7 *Wimblebury* (Hunslet 3839/1956), as a spare engine to cover servicing or failure of the diesel. *Mike Wood*

Below:
Cannock & Rugeley Colliery Co's Peckett 0-6-0ST (786/1899) was formerly Rowlands No 6 before becoming CRC No 3. At the end of a busy week the fire was dropped at Cannock Wood and *Progress* retired for a rest and possibly replacement of a firebar, the new one being carried to the rear of the locomotive. Banks of accumulated ash piled up on both sides of the track.

Above:
Rules were never broken on the CRC system, but could often be severely bent. Having been engaged in tracklaying during the day, the uphill return to the colliery with the truck was hard work but was, fortunately, eased by hitching a lift behind No 7 *Wimblebury* returning with its van after taking a load of coal down to Hednesford. It is to be wondered what the Health & Safety Executive of today would have made of the procedure.

Below:
Loaded three-hopper flat wagons are again featured, this time on the CRC line as veteran 0-6-0ST No 1 *Marquess*, built by the Lilleshall Co in 1867, sauntered along at Rawnsley in 1957. These wagons took coal down to the canal interchange at Hednesford basin, where the coal would be lifted and tipped into waiting narrow boats for distribution throughout the Midlands. *Geoff Bannister*

Above:
CRC No 9 *Cannock Wood* was built by the London Brighton & South Coast Railway in 1877 as 'E1' class B110 *Burgundy*. It was sold to the CRC in 1927. Withdrawn in 1963 with a defective firebox, it was moved to the Hednesford Railway Preservation Society. When given notice to quit its premises, the society could not meet the deadline. Cannock Wood was towed back to Rawnsley by the NCB who later generously moved it to Chasewater on 20 October 1970. In September 1978 the locomotive moved to the East Somerset Railway. It is photographed here at Rawnsley shed.

Below:
Another pretty little 0-4-0ST with a spark-arrester chimney worked at Heath Hayes. It is here portrayed taking water at the colliery. Output from the 'Fair Lady' was dropped down beneath the Norton Road bridge to sidings where a '4F' 0-6-0 exchanged wagons daily. The coal went through Norton Canes at 12.5pm, the '4F', known as 'the Blackie', appearing as schoolchildren came out of school and enjoyed being bathed in steam and smoke at Norton Bridge. With 'snap' bags hanging on the locomotive's handbrake, it was obviously not yet time for serious eating.

Above:

Passengers at Penkridge for Stafford talked on the platform surrounded by tubs of colourful and scented flowers. Stafford's No 42603 paused at the station, then continued on its way to Birmingham with a short parcels train. The up platform overlooked the parish church and the quiet little market town. No 42603 was built in December 1936 and withdrawn in May 1963.

Below:

Littleton colliery, Huntington (Cannock), was Cannock Chase's last working colliery, formerly producing much coal for power station use. After record breaking productivity, the colliery was closed on 10 December 1993. In better times 'Austerity' No 2 had the attention of three shunters in the reception sidings. The bunker of the Hunslet (3772/1952) was loaded with Littleton's best, and the locomotive is about to pull out a load of power station coal to be taken to the BR interchange at Penkridge, 3½ miles away. The number of shunters reflected the traffic some 20 years ago, the colliery having an active fleet of eight steam locomotives.

Above left:
Hunslet No 2 is pictured standing outside the elegantly-gabled shed at Littleton in an age when the depot had a traditional apex roof. The cab of a small Hunslet was strangely posed between the tracks. The roof was removed about 1951/52 when the water tank was resited on the new flat roof. *Norman Glover/Mike Wood's Collection*

Left:
Loads down to Penkridge, empties up to Littleton; Chase collieries were situated on the high ground which made for economical working of loaded trains downhill. Passing through delightful farmland up a 1 in 60 gradient No 4 *Robert Nelson* (Hunslet 1800/1936) is seen at Mansty Farm with a raft of empties bound for the colliery.

Above:
The 'Big Engine', No 5 *Littleton* (Manning Wardle 2018/1922), and No 2 in repose outside the modified shed.

Right:
The last steam run at Littleton, thunderous and spectacular, occurred on 18 February 1978. Hunslet No 7 (1752/1943) is seen approaching the colliery with empties. Within a week the locomotive was transferred to Bold colliery, St Helens, where it continued in NCB service, where it was named *Robert*. *Mike Wood*

Stafford

Stafford, at the junction of the Trent Valley line to Euston and the branch to Wolverhampton, Birmingham and the Midlands, was always an important and busy railway centre. Two branch lines went their separate ways just north of the solid Victorian station, left (after passing W. G. Bagnall's Castle Locomotive Works) to Wellington and Shrewsbury, and right to Uttoxeter and Derby. Both branches, long closed, ran through delightful rolling countryside and pleasant villages. Just a few miles north, at Norton Bridge, a line diverged eastwards giving access to the Potteries and Manchester.

Stafford shed (5C) hosted over the years North Western, Midland and North Stafford (Knotty) locomotives, whilst an interesting assortment of Great Northern power entered the town via Uttoxeter. As a youngster, the author witnessed the last work of the ex-LNWR 'Prince of Wales' class as Nos 25648 *Queen of the Belgians* and 25673 *Lusitania* were long-time residents of 5C. Postwar, the 'Duchesses', colourless, drab and filthy looked massive in their streamlined form. No 6243 *City of Lancaster* was the last, in May 1949, to be defrocked, whilst Edge Hill's last

'Claughton', No 6004, passed through occasionally on freight.

On transfer to a school in Stafford in 1948, the author saw, in addition to the procession of Fowler and Stanier designed locomotives, 'A4' No 60034 *Lord Faringdon* and 'Merchant Navy' No 35017 *Belgian Marine* working north on the down 'Royal Scot' whilst temporarily allocated to the LMR for the Locomotive Exchanges — trials which were to help in the preparation of data for the new Standard locomotive designs. With the decline of the 'Princes', modern versions of the Midland '2P' 4-4-0 took over the local services and semi-fasts to Manchester and Rugby. These were later followed by the excellent Fowler 2-6-4Ts. The 'Super D' was the standard freight locomotive, with Stanier '8Fs' arriving as the 0-8-0s declined. '4Fs' were common from Burton and shunting was firmly in the hands of '3F' 'Jinty' 0-6-0Ts. Such was the variety of locomotive to be seen in 1948 that after only a few weeks a new notebook was required!

Below:
No 49234 headed past Queensville on the morning freight, shortly to be overtaken by a Class 5 on the 'main'.

The Stafford & Uttoxeter Railway

The submissions for the Stafford & Uttoxeter line were filed at Stafford on 30 November 1861. The bill came before Parliament in February 1862 and received the Royal Assent on 29 July 1862. The promoters saw lucrative potential in conveying cattle from Wales to the dairy-intensive North Midlands, and transport for shoes and salt from Stafford to markets in the east. The line was taken over by the Great Northern from 1 August 1881, with GNR (LNER after 1923) locomotives being regular motive power on the line. Passenger services into Stafford terminated in the northern bay, with general interchange of freight wagons past the station in the extensive southern yards. The rich pasturage and rolling countryside of North Staffordshire ensured regular milk traffic; the GNR picking it up with the daily milk express timed to leave Stafford Common station at 5.40pm to King's Cross, empties returning early the following morning.

Right:
Intense activity at the northern end of the Stafford station of yesteryear. The north end gantries stood imposing their semaphore authority over the main lines where a mixed up freight awaited clearance to the south. With the 'Bay' peg pulled off, Ivatt 'J6' 0-6-0 No 3623 eased its venerable three-coach rake (with look-out extensions at each end) towards Bagnall's Bridge on its up journey to Uttoxeter and Derby. Whilst it is true that up trains passed through Exeter St Davids in opposite directions, up trains at Stafford did so but a few feet apart and using the same track, as seen in this classic Percy Kendrick shot. The light '4F' was waiting to cross to the shed (off picture right), while the 'Knotty' tank at the end of the down bay waited to follow the 0-6-0's path to the refuge of 5C.
Percy Kendrick/Phil Jones' Collection

Right:
A mixed freight for the Stafford & Uttoxeter, with two 'salts' behind the van, left Stafford, crossing the main lines, hauled by 'E1' 2-4-0 N0 868 and 'J3' 0-6-0 No 4151.
Locomotive & General/Phil Jones' Collection

The Last Train on the S&U
23 March 1957

The last train to run over the Stafford & Uttoxeter, known locally as the 'Clog & Knocker' (no doubt from the acoustics when climbing the steep banks along part of the line), was photographed by the *Stafford Newsletter* cameraman on 23 March 1957 passing beneath Stafford Common station. Walsall Ryecroft's Ivatt '2MT' 2-6-2T No 41224 was impressively turned out at the head of the three-coach push-pull set. The last rite, SLS special from Birmingham, was fully patronised, with many would-be passengers at Stafford disappointed and unable to travel. The eight shillings (40p) fare from Birmingham seemed to be a bargain for a ride over the beautiful line. To allow passage of the train, the right of way had to be cleared of bush growth and young trees. Sadly missed since its closure to passenger traffic on 4 December 1939, villagers turned out in numbers at the stations and in gardens to witness the passing of the final train. The *Railway Preservation Forum* magazine featured, in reminiscence, an article by 'Onlooker' in its summer 1962 edition, an article which was written with great feeling for the line, its interesting locomotives and the English language:

'For 11 years this line has been derelict; weeds, bushes and thick undergrowth have sprung up along the permanent way, but the rusty single track can be traced as it threads its way through 13 miles of the prettiest scenery in Staffordshire, passing Sandon Park, ivy covered Chartley Castle, and along the lovely valley of the Trent. To the visitor, the line presents a silent picture of decay, abandonment and sheer beauty. Here can be discovered a platelayer's hut surrounded by a carpet of bluebells, a cabin housing a nest of young swallows, and a deep cutting where silver birch trees hang low over the track, and where moss and lichen drip water on to the rocks. There are scenes, too, which mar the beauty of the old line — the blackened horseshoe nailed to the burned-out shell of a hut, its contents strewn over a large area; the deserted cottage with its shutters banging in the wind, and the crumbling platforms and tottering buildings which can be seen at every station.'

Thank you, dear 'Onlooker', whoever you are. Sheer magic! And so, too, were the steam locomotives and little trains of the S&U.

Top: This print is included to lay one of David Preston's ghosts to rest. David recently wrote an excellent article on Stafford in *Steam Days* (September 1992). I quote from his final paragraph: 'I never saw a non-LMS type, other than Standards or WDs, in Stafford, although I have seen reports in *Trains Illustrated* of occasional WR diversions and someone once said he had seen an LNER 'B1' on a Whit Monday.' I cannot confirm that No 61233 was photographed on a Whit Monday, but the 'B1' was seen on this up freight passing the 'UNI' works; a filthy locomotive but, nonetheless, a rare event at Stafford.

Above: No 46253 *City of St Albans* is pictured bursting out of Shugborough tunnel with the down 'Caledonian'. The architecture of the tunnel had to be in keeping with that of the large Shugborough estate.

Left: Walsall Ryecroft (3C) provided the motive power to haul the final train — an SLS special — over the Stafford & Uttoxeter line. Immaculate Ivatt 2-6-2T No 41224 was bringing an era to a close as it passed through Stafford Common station. *Stafford Newsletter/Phil Jones' Collection*

Above:
Cousins in the Stafford gloom as No 45526 overtook 'Royal Scot' 4-6-0 No 46166 *The London Rifle Brigade* leaving with an afternoon train to Shrewsbury. No 45526 *Morecambe & Heysham* is holding the main line and accelerating its Euston-Carlisle express after the Queensville speed restriction. No 45526 was built in March 1933, rebuilt with a 2A taper boiler in February 1947 and withdrawn in October 1964. No 46166's curriculum vitae was very similar: new October 1930; reboilered January 1945; and withdrawn September 1964.

Right:
An incoming arrival from Shrewsbury at Stafford's canopied platform 6. No 42389 was one of Stafford's immaculately kept Fowler 2-6-4Ts and was photographed as passengers detrained and parcels from the front vehicle were taken by trolley to the parcels area —possibly for forwarding southwards from platform 1. No 42389 was new in June 1933 and withdrawn in March 1963.

Centre right:
Crewe North's No 46200 *The Princess Royal*, standing tall against the tiered deciduous woodland of Shugborough, crossed to take the divergent slow line through Milford as a prelude to its Stafford stop on a Euston-Liverpool express. The locomotive was built in July 1933 and withdrawn in November 1962.

Below:
Simply disdaining its light two-coach parcels working, 'Royal Scot' 4-6-0 No 46115 *Scots Guardsman* shot away from its Stafford stop on probably ¼ regulator and 15% cut off as it left for the north on a wintry, but sunny, day.

Above left:
'Crab' 2-6-0 No 42943 enveloped the 5C coaler in a blanket of steam and smoke, whilst at the same time helping to keep the water column from freezing with steam from its opened cocks as it prepared to move off shed. The severe winter of 1963 was a cause of much disruption as diesel train heating boilers failed and steam substitutes had to be found by Crewe North.

Left:
Strangely diverted to the down slow, No 46233 *Duchess of Sutherland* showed a nonchalant dissatisfaction with the insult, its driver slamming the 16-coach Glasgow express northbound past the Universal Grinding Wheel's spacious car park in an attempt to minimise loss of time to Crewe over the speed-restricted slow line. The locomotive was built in July 1933 and was withdrawn (for preservation) in February 1964.

Top:
In what could be a modern version of a Hans Anderson fairytale, No 46209, again of Camden, undertook bridge raising activity at Stafford in preparation for electrification. 'The Princess and the crane' was, however, a reality as *Princess Beatrice* was whisked out of Crewe North — probably a clandestine operation — for this Sunday event. This was surely the most bizarre 'Princess' duty ever. But, again, the 5A shedmaster was a devotee of the big '8Ps' even in decline and would do anything to get them 'on the road'. An enthusiast and a gentleman indeed.

Above:
'Princesses' in decline. The large noticeboard confirmed that 'A new station is being built here in connection with London Midland electrification'. An immaculate No 46207 *Princess Arthur of Connaught* of Camden (1B) passed majestically through the station on its afternoon Euston-Liverpool express (1K32). A huge demolition crane has been erected, ready for work over the entrance to the old station — a building soon to be no more.

The nameplate from 'Royal Scot' No 46138 *The London Irish Rifleman*.

Above left:
Spotless 'Jubilee' No 45733 *Novelty*, a former Bushbury favourite but now carrying a 1A shedplate, passed Stafford No 6 signalbox with an up fitted freight diverted to the freight lines to the west of the station. No 6 controlled the entrance to the shed. The elegant canopy over platform 6 has already gone, and a temporary materials and workmen's shed has come to grace the platform, which remains in use for locals to Shrewsbury.

Left:
A temporary overbridge servicing the local platform 6, the 'Salop', overshadowed a Sunday stop for the unique No 46106 *Gordon Highlander*, which ran with BR Standard-type smoke deflectors. Rubble and turmoil everywhere surrounded the 'Scot', which was engaged on a Glasgow-Birmingham service. No 46106 was constructed in August 1927 and withdrawn from active service in December 1962.

Above:
No 46114 *Coldstream Guardsman* of Crewe North looked as though it had just come off a muddy assault course; definitely not passing muster roll for duty outside Buckingham Palace! The train was halted at Newport and comprised the normal three coaches for this service. The service often had locomotives recently ex-works as a further variation on the running-in theme. *Hugh Ballantyne*

Above:
A light engine run to Stafford was often undertaken to run-in locomotives which had just been through heavy repair at Crewe Works. Wellingborough-based Standard Class 9F No 92021, built as a Crosti variant but rebuilt in simple form, was seen outside 5C awaiting return to Crewe for a final assessment and then return to Wellingborough for more heavy duty.

Below:
Another variation was to send the locomotive for a trip in revenue service. Stanier '8F' No 48005 was given the task of hauling a train of pre-laid concrete sections down the Trent Valley main line for weekend tracklaying somewhere south of Stafford. The photograph was taken on the up slow line at Stockton Lane.

W.G. Bagnall of Stafford

The Castle Engine Works of W. G. Bagnall was established in 1876 when William Gordon Bagnall and his partner William Hill went their separate ways and Bagnall took complete control of the company. Bagnall offered machinery and locomotives for sale, a line in which the company specialised for almost 100 years. Seeing a market for small locomotives suitable for lightly laid track, Bagnall offered a wide variety of types and gauges. The company soon had a thriving export business, particularly to India. As the firm prospered and expanded with engineering and design flair apparent, larger units were offered, culminating in the two-metre gauge 2-8-2 tender locomotives for the Sao Paulo Pararna Railway in Brazil. Similar 'Special YD' locomotives also went to the South Central Railway of India. These weighed 101 tons and had a tractive effort of 27,616lb.

Opportunities for the domestic market were also exploited; Pannier tanks were constructed for the Great Western Railway and 25 'Jinty' 0-6-0Ts (Nos 16535-49/675-84) for the LMS, with two going to the Northern Counties Committee in Northern Ireland (Nos 18 and 19).

Bagnall locomotives were simple, robust and long-lived. Many are still operational overseas. It was fitting that the 100th meeting of the Continental Railway Circle (Midlands), held at Stafford on 10 November 1993, featured an illustrated address on Bagnall's works and its locomotives by Allan C. Baker, co-author of *Bagnall Locomotives — A Pictorial Album of Bagnall Narrow Gauge Locomotives*. Allan, a native of North Staffordshire, followed an engineering and management career with British Railways, becoming Depot Manager at Finsbury Park where he oversaw the day-to-day provision of 'Deltic' power for the East Coast route, prior to moving on to Stratford. A life-long student of the products of the Castle Engine Works, he purchased the 0-4-0ST *Hawarden* (WB2623/1940) from the Shelton Iron & Steel Works, Etruria (Stoke-on-Trent), and ran her for almost 10 years, relinquishing her to the Foxfield on his move south in 1981.

Below:
Hawarden was pictured on the toughest job in the works — the slag run. Molten slag was dumped from the side tippler wagon. Allan C. Baker's evocative and atmospheric photograph was taken during his locomotive's days at Shelton on 7 May 1969. The 15in x 12in cylindered standard Bagnall was the last steam locomotive delivered to Shelton and worked until March 1972. *Allan C. Baker*

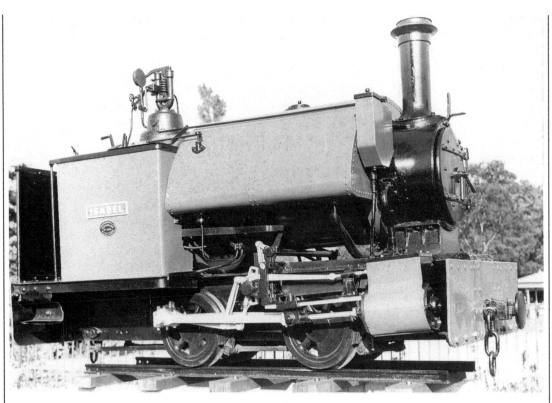

Isabel (Bagnall 1491/1897) was sold to the Cliffe Hill granite quarries at Markfield, Leicestershire, as a 2ft gauge, 7in cylinder model. In a long working life she wore out three boilers, before being returned to Stafford in March 1952 where she was mechanically rebuilt by the firm's apprentices. The locomotive was displayed on a plinth at the works for Coronation Year (1953). On the cessation of locomotive work at Bagnalls in 1963 she was released for display on a plinth between the station and Victoria Park. After considerable deterioration she returned to the works in 1977 where she was the last locomotive to receive attention. The little locomotive has recently been returned to steam duties at Amerton Farm, just a few miles from her birthplace, where *Isabel* will shortly celebrate her centenary.

Centre left:
A Bagnall advertising postcard.

Below left:
A Bagnall maker's plate. *Mike Wood.*

The Magic of Badnall Wharf

By early 1959, surplus track at Winsford (Over Wharton branch) and at Badnall Wharf (near Eccleshall) was used to store many withdrawn locomotives prior to sale and breaking up for scrap. At Winsford, several ex-London, Tilbury & Southend 0-6-2Ts were lined up, but further south, at Badnall, a magical collection of varied power came together.

Representative classes from the LT&S, Somerset & Dorset and Lancashire & Yorkshire railways shared the company of ex-Midland and LMS types. The author was permitted access, by courtesy of the Area Manager's Office at Crewe, through a one day extension to his lineside permit. For a time, railway travellers between Stafford and Crewe were treated to a real show, a railway museum in miniature. Perhaps most interesting were the two ex-S&D steam Sentinels and the varied collection of ex-L&Y 2-4-2Ts (with round top and Belpaire fireboxes, extended smokeboxes and bunkers). A prospective buyer with £20,000 in his pocket could have considerably extended the National Collection. But time ran out and the magic of 1959 soon disappeared.

Locomotives at Badnall Wharf in 1959 included: Nos 41078, 41156, 41158, 41797, 41724, 41936, 47190, 47191, 43248, 43339, 43419, 43619, 43630, 43631, 43674, 47247 (condensing), 50831, 50865, 52399, 58066, 58171, 58196, 58198.

Left:
'Jubilee' 4-6-0 No 45571 *South Africa*, light engine to Crewe, passes the parade at Badnall Wharf.

Left:
Sadly withdrawn and awaiting the cutter's torch, redundant locomotives displayed a good cross-section of ex-LMS motive power in a free half-mile display. The closest locomotives in this photograph were, left to right, Nos 51257, 43631, 41724, two 2-4-2Ts hidden by wagons, 51424 and 50646.

Above:

Radstock's four-coupled shunters, built in 1885 and 1895, were considered life-expired by the S&D, which ordered two diminutive Sentinel 0-4-0 replacements in 1929. The low height of Nos 47190/91 was necessary to allow clearance beneath Tyning Bridge, near Radstock signalbox. The pair were withdrawn in 1959 and were certainly the rarest machines in the line-up.

Below:

The tender water tank of 'Royal Scot' 4-6-0 No 46130 *The West Yorkshire Regiment* was approaching full as the lightly loaded Manchester-Birmingham service traversed Whitmore troughs. The control hut and water purification facility (left) had just been passed by an '8F', the guard's van of the latter train being seen in the distance.

Crewe and Stoke

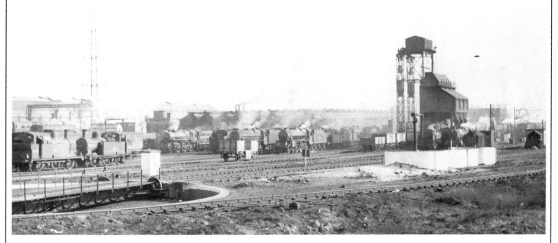

Above:
A well-stocked Crewe South (5B) was visible over the turntable as Jim Hardy lined up this shot for posterity. Jim, then working in Crewe Control, was thus on home ground and portrayed the character of South to perfection. Four 'Jinty' 0-6-0Ts for shunting the extensive yards were on shed, with a varied selection of tender locomotives.
Jim Hardy

Below:
In the wired era. Nos 46237 *City of Bristol* and 46127 *The Old Contemptibles* prepared to leave Crewe, always a traffic bottleneck, so allowing access for other trains which were probably held outside the station. No 46127 was an old friend of the author's, and was seen when he was young and on a week's holiday to North Wales near Abergele. During the week *The Old Contemptibles* worked turn about with No 46112 *Sherwood Forester* on the up 'Irish Mail'. At that time both locomotives had recently been fitted with their new type 2A taper boiler; No 46112 in September 1943 and No 46127 in August 1944. *Jim Hardy*

Left:
Crewe North (5A) had a smaller allocation than South, mainly of express passenger locomotives. The depot had a strong allocation of Pacifics for the heaviest duties, their sternest tasks probably being the heavy overnight Euston-Perth sleepers, which were often loaded to 15 or 16 coaches to be taken over Shap and Beattock. For this duty the locomotives had to be in excellent mechanical condition. They continued to perform the duty right up until final withdrawal in 1964. One power group down were the 'Scots', rebuilt 'Jubilees' and 'Patriots', which were considered all one class, although the last-named had cylinders ½ in less in diameter. No 46155 *The Lancer* was seen under steam at 5A. *Jim Hardy*

Left:
A senior fitter looked on as No 70023 *Venus* was put through a boiler washout at Crewe North. The exhaust steam injector was getting a good dose of accumulated filth from the boiler's 'mud-hole'. After refitting the mud-hole cover, the boiler would be refilled and the locomotive put back into service.

Left:
Photographic facilities were made available at 5A, by the kind co-operation of the shedmaster, for special occasions and last runs. On the occasion of *Blink Bonny* visiting the shed, the shedmaster laid on an informative guided tour by a senior driver for this visitor and the photographer. The walk enabled the author to photograph three superbly-kept machines: No 45512 *Bunsen* (12B) which was situated over the inspection pit, flanked by Nos 60051 (left) and 70004 *William Shakespeare*.

Above:
No 60051 *Blink Bonny* was the selected locomotive to haul the 'South Yorkshireman No 2' railtour, which was a combined Halifax Railfans and Gresley Society visit to Derby and Crewe Works on 18 April 1964. The locomotive was cleaned overnight by 'volunteers' from the societies' membership, who did an excellent job on the racehorse.

Below:
No 70050 *Firth of Clyde* took centre stage at its home depot in this photograph. The locomotive was one of the last 10 'Britannias' to be ordered (in 1953). In common with the rest of the batch it had a modified flush-sided tender holding nine tons of coal. The tender was additionally fitted with a coal pusher. The cab design was also modified to cut down draughts and a speedometer was driven from the left rear coupled crank pin. The locomotives also had plain section coupling rods. *Jim Hardy*

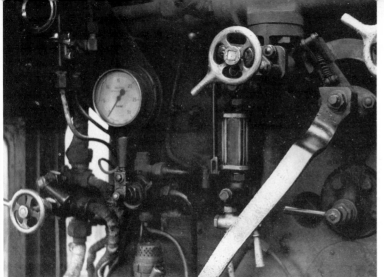

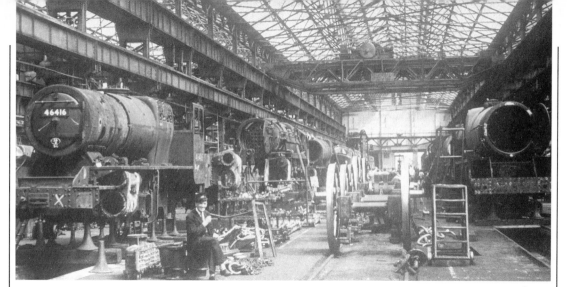

Above:

Bill, the Crewe Works' guide, was resting his feet awhile as he waited for the visitors to go down the erection shop between the loco-motives and return up the next aisle. The popular and informative visits, for so long a Sunday ritual at the works, gave an interesting insight into locomotive technology and construction.

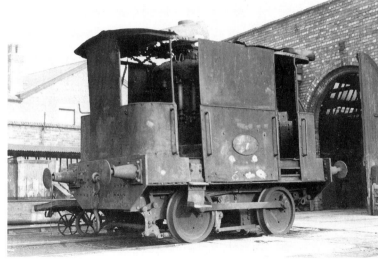

Right:

Not an ex-works paint job, this veteran semi-derelict vertical boilered tram engine survived around the paint shop area for a considerable time. It was seen in several locations over a number of visits; the author was never able to satisfy his curiosity as to its origin or usage.

Right:

Class 5s Nos 45374, 44781 and 45455 (12A), having just emerged from the paint shop in 'economy' unlined black, awaited removal to Crewe North or South depots (both were used) to prepare for steaming and running-in trips. Yet later, locomotives were turned out in 'patch paint' livery, where perhaps only the repaired feature, such as smokebox or firebox, would be repainted.

I never saw a newly-painted 'Princess' or 'Duchess' at Crewe Works, but I did manage a portrait of No 6233 after she had been withdrawn and cosmetically repainted in LMS maroon in readiness for display at Butlins. However, Holbeck's 'Jubilee' No 45565 *Victoria* proved to be an excellent substitute, sparkling in the superb BR lined green livery.

Below:
Over the years Crewe Works used a wide variety of motive power for its shunting duties. On this visit there were three shunters on view: an Aspinall Class 27 0-6-0 with round-top firebox and short smokebox, its weather sheet prominent on the cab roof; No 52093, introduced in 1889 with roundtop firebox and extended smokebox; and a '3F' 0-6-0T. All had been repainted for works service.

Above:
On the author's visit to the Over Wharton branch to view the ex-LT&S 0-6-2Ts No 41985 was the best of the bunch so far as general external condition was concerned. In mediocre light, the locomotive was given the privilege of a side ¾ portrait from his trusted Selfix Special with its superb Ross Xpres 3.8 lens.

Below:
Florence colliery No 2 (Bagnall 3059/1953) was a late Stafford product. It was sold new to the colliery where it gave excellent service at its Longton home. No 2 was a standard Bagnall 16in x 24in outside-cylinder 0-6-0ST built to a 1944 design, which was produced in numbers until 1955. The locomotive was fitted with a Giesl ejector in 1966. Transferred to Cadley Hill colliery, it was preserved at Shackerstone on that colliery's closure. *Allan C. Baker*

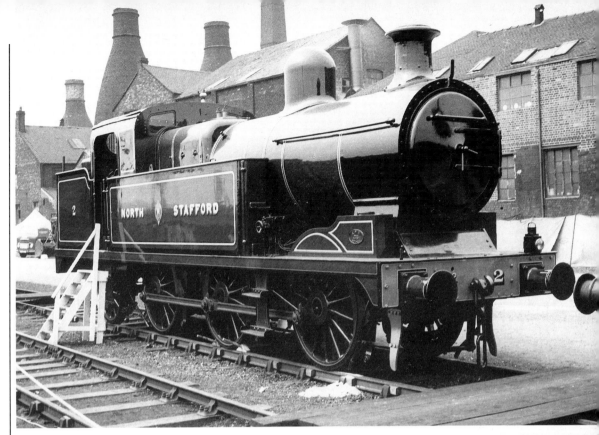

Above left:
Nos 75030 and 45038 lined up with other Stanier-designed locomotives at Stoke MPD towards the end of steam operation at 5D. Stoke's locomotives once had the luxury of a magnificent roundhouse shed.

Left:
No 790, the fabled *Hardwicke*, achieved its fame and ultimate preservation by being a West Coast representative in the Railways Races to the North on 22 August 1895. *Jim Hardy*

Above:
During 1960 the City of Stoke-on-Trent celebrated its Jubilee. Included in the Jubilee display was a line up of locomotives associated with the city, and footplate inspections were allowed. The LNWR 2-2-2 *Cornwall* and 2-4-0 No 790 *Hardwicke* represented the older power, the 'Knotty' was represented by No 2, the LMS by No 46254 *City of Stoke-on-Trent* — the Crewe North shedmaster's favourite locomotive. No 2 was then working at Mossley Common colliery and was specially repainted for the occasion. *Jim Hardy*

Above:
Fowler parallel-boilered 2-6-4T No 42381 emerged from the tunnel into a wonderland of sunshine, elegant trees and superb railway architecture as it prepared to pull up for its stop at Oakamoor. North Staffordshire has much magnificent scenery and the unique North Staffordshire Railway architecture made a superb background for photographing a working railway. It is a pity that more has not been published portraying this beautiful area. *Jim Hardy*

Above:
Ivatt 2-6-2T No 41241 of 84H (Wellington) attracted little passenger traffic at Audlem on the NSR Stoke-on-Trent-Market Drayton line. Audlem, like other stations on the line, closed as the route's economic viability declined. A small section of track was kept open from Silverdale to Madeley for merry-go-round coal traffic from Silverdale colliery principally to Fiddlers Ferry power station near Warrington. With the colliery's closure on 10 December 1993, total closure of the line seems inevitable. *Hugh Ballantyne*

Below:
Ryecroft depot (3C) rostered Stanier 2-6-4T No 42627 to haul the SLS 'North Staffordshire' railtour (W725), which toured several lines including a visit to Caldon quarry near Waterhouses. The Stanier was well away from its customary haunts, but performed well and posed for the obligatory photo stops. The white-coated wagons (left) had obviously seen much service in the quarry. The quarry's water tower is seen above the passengers on the right. *Geoff Bannister*

Above:
Having made the journey from Stafford over the S&U, 'D2' 4-4-0 No 4365 stood at Uttoxeter to exchange passengers as a North Stafford 0-6-2T eased a loaded van (possibly containing milk churns) to the rear of the Derby-bound train. Three tank wagons are visible in the distance beneath the platform canopy. The station sign clearly instructed passengers from the north to change at Uttoxeter for Stafford, Ashbourne, the Churnet Valley and Burton. *Locomotive & General*

Below:
This Stanier '8F' paused for water at Uttoxeter as it hauled a coal train from Stoke south. During the operation the starter signal was released, then the distant was raised indicating a clear line well ahead. Of interest is the klaxon horn seen beyond the fireman, for long-range communication from the station or signalbox. Only the through road from Stoke to Derby is left of the complex triangular station — a unique and delightfully detailed period piece of great charm.

Above:
Withdrawn and stored locomotives at Uttoxeter included '2P' 4-4-0 No 40653, which was withdrawn in 1959. Built in 1939 as part of Lot No 76 (which was for 30 4-4-0s), No 40653 was one of two fitted with Dabeg feedwaters heaters as an experiment in increasing boiler efficiency. No 40633 was Dabeg fitted in November 1933 and No 40653 was similarly dealt with in January 1934. The experiment was not adopted for general use, thankfully, as it marred the aesthetically clean lines of the LMS version of the Johnson '2P'. *Jim Hardy*

Below:
There was plenty of footplate co-operation from the crew of No 49281 (Buxton — 9D) featured at the head of a very mixed freight train to Ashbourne. The first vehicle was a a six-wheel milk tank.
Jim Hardy

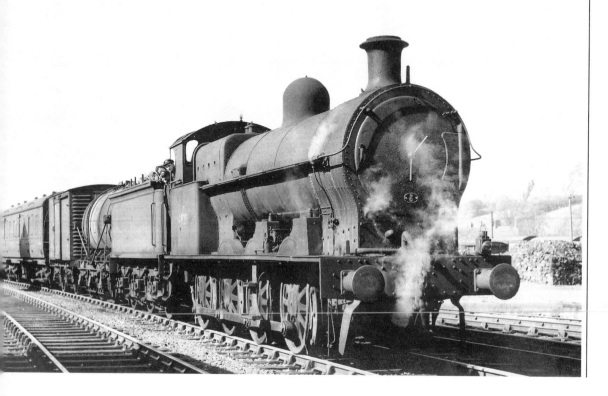

Burton upon Trent

Burton was synonymous with the production of quality beers, its needs being met by the Midland, London & North Western, Great Northern and North Staffordshire railways. Motive power through the town was varied, from the huge Beyer-Peacock 2-6-6-2 working coal trains to Birmingham and beyond to diminutive Deeley 0-4-0Ts and Sentinel shunters. The town was graced by the passage of the 'Devonian' from Bradford (Forster Square) to Paignton at 12.30pm, although the train stopped in the town only on its northbound journey. Industrial steam locomotives operated on the internal systems of several breweries, Bass being the largest operator with lesser fleets run by Worthington, Ind Coope & Marston, Thompson & Evershed. There were also industrial locomotives at the Branston Artificial Silk Co and Lloyds Foundry, while Truman, Hanbury & Buxton used the services of a small Peckett 0-4-0ST.

Bass, having origins in 1777, grew into a huge 800-acre complex with 16 miles of track and running powers over a further 10 miles of LMS/BR track. Up to 1,000 wagon movements could be expected a day, with loads being taken out, empties brought in and internal movement of hops, malt, etc. Trainloads for distribution were substantial, the most famous being the 'Scotch' special north to Leeds and Scotland via the S&C. Several road crossings in the town saw considerable traffic by rail, the neat signalboxes

Below:
With 7ft 0½in driving wheels, No 40396 was designed in 1882, the class being rebuilt by the Midland from 1910 onwards. Withdrawn with chimney bagged, it lined up with other similar power at 17B (Burton). Beyond the '2P', the depot's freight power, including No 43188, was still in steam. The rapid proliferation of DMUs quickly displaced such elderly passenger locomotives throughout the country.

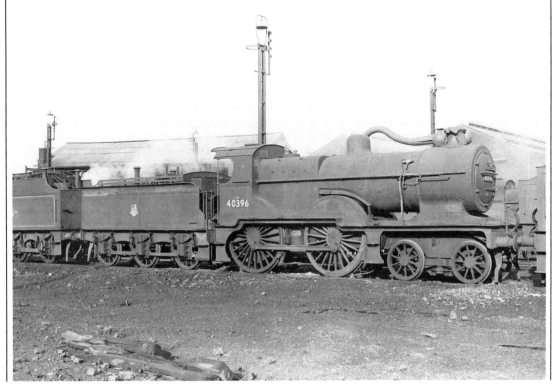

using both semaphore and horizontal cross-bar signals.

The Bass fleet of small 0-4-0STs was a delight; clean and polished in crimson brown with copper-capped chimneys and brass domes. Over-large buffers seemed an anachronism, but these were necessary to prevent derailments on the sharp curves throughout the system.

The local firm of Thornewill & Wareham supplied Bass's first locomotive in 1871, and a second 0-4-0WT strangely being numbered 224 some two years later. Larger well tanks followed, of the 'Faery' and 'Triangle' classes, forming a fleet of 13 by 1890. North British built the larger 'A' class between 1899 and 1913; these were Nos 1, 2, 4, 10 and 11. The North British engines remained until the end of steam operation, supplemented by Class B No 3 (formerly No 13). This had been built as a well tank in 1890, rebuilt as a saddle tank in 1909 and again in 1924 with a driver's cab. No 9, of the 'Faery' class, and the visitors saloon have been preserved at the Bass Museum of Brewing. The saloon, built in 1899, came from the Manchester Ship Canal Co. They make a delightful display in the museum.

Burton BR shed (17B) was host to a variety of power, mainly '3F' and '4F' 0-6-0s and smaller 0-6-0T and 0-4-0T shunters. 2-6-4Ts serviced Leicester line locals and late 1961 saw an influx of 'Jubilees' — some already withdrawn — with a further seven arriving between December 1961 and April 1964. The useful '2P' 4-4-0s were also used on passenger services, but also appeared on freight turns as required. The early '2P' 4-4-0s, with their 7ft 0½in driving wheels, visited Walsall regularly during the author's youth. They had to shunt their own returning wagons. Whilst ungainly, they did prove Midland flexibility.

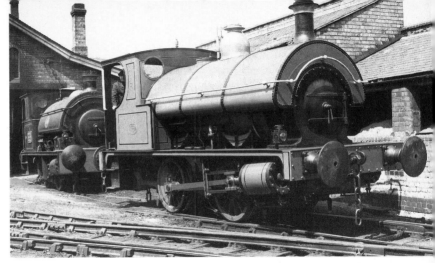

Below left:
North British-built 'A' class No 11 (of 1899) and Sentinel diesel No 12 were temporarily held up by 'B' class 0-4-0ST No 3, built in 1890 by Thornewill & Wareham, about to go on shed for the weekend.

Right:
Always immaculately kept, Bass No 2 and Worthington No 16 lined up outside the shed. The brown-lake of Bass locomotives complemented and contrasted with the deep blue of their Worthington counterparts. Worthington also used simple and unsightly Planet diesels for light shunting duties. *Hugh Ballantyne*

Centre right:
Pretty little outside-cylinder Bass 'A' class No 1 went about its distribution duties in the extensive brewing complex. The North British-built tank shunted empty five-plank wagons for loading barrels, with vans for kegs and crated beers. *Jim Hardy*

Below right:
Bass 'A' class No 10 and the 1889-built saloon were photographed on a visit to the brewery by the Stafford Railway Circle. The little 0-4-0ST had 14in x 21in cylinders, 3ft 6in driving wheels on a 6ft 6in wheelbase and weighed 23 ½ tons empty. Note the coal stacked in the front of the left-hand side of the cab, and the outside brakeman's seat on the saloon.

Class A No 2 was photographed by Allsopp's Crossing, which was controlled by the stylish little signalbox set off by finials. Boxes of various styles and shapes to fit the available space were a feature of the system. The train of barley hoppers was watched by the shunter with his shunting pole at the ready.

The internal system was controlled by upper and lower quadrant semaphore signals, and by the cross-bar signals; one of the latter is seen by the box. The single track to Allsopp's can be seen crossing at 180° beneath the third wagon. The signal was set to allow passage of the train, but against traffic on the Allsopp line. No 11 was the duty engine in this view. The three-storey building on the right was later modified to form the Bass Museum of Brewing, displaying a fascinating collection of literature, photographs and relics which is well worth a visit.

The Tutbury 'Jenny'

The Tutbury 'Jenny' was a little train serving the delightful country between Burton and Tutbury, a distance of some 5½ miles encompassing the catchment areas of the rivers Trent and Dove. Intermediate stations served villages, farmsteads and cottages along the line's sickle-shaped route. The line initially headed east from Burton, before swinging north then northwest to Tutbury, with stations at Horninglow, Stretton & Clay Mills and Rolleston on Dove.

The service ran for over a century, commencing in 1848 and saw a considerable variety of motive power — North Stafford, LMS and BR —over the years. The push-pull 'Jenny' was driven from the motor compartment of the end coach for the propelled return journey from Tutbury. Although two coaches were the normal load, it was not unknown for the train to be formed of one or three coaches. Final motive power came in the form of Ivatt tanks; the final train running on 11 June 1960. Tributes to mark the closure of the service were chalked all over No 41277. The intermediate stations, closed on 1 January 1949 to regular traffic, came back to life as locals witnessed the passing of the final 'Jenny'. The 'Jenny' was an institution, its several daily journeys a ritual; now, alas, it is but a distant memory.

Above:
Ivatt '2MT' 2-6-2T No 41277 was photographed at Tutbury being prepared for its return run to Burton at 4.37pm. The Tutbury platform was graced by beautiful cast lamps, silent and watchful platform sentries, as the tank simmered peacefully at the rear of its little train. The fireman would be separated from the company of his driver during the 5 ½ mile amble back to Burton. *Hugh Ballantyne*

Above left:
Cadley Hill colliery, a few miles from Burton, was the last bastion of steam in the area. Cadley Hill No 1 (Hunslet 3851/1962) was bathed in steam when seen passing beneath the Burton-Swadlincote roadbridge with a rake of loaded coal wagons being taken out of the colliery's storage sidings for sale and distribution. *Mike Wood*

Left:
An interesting line up of Cadley Hill power outside the loco-motive shed, featuring, from left to right, RSH 0-6-ST *Progress* (7298/1946), 'Austerity' 0-6-0ST No 1 and outside-cylinder Bagnall 0-6-0ST *Empress* (3061/1954). The name-plates on Progress were formerly carried by Cannock & Rugeley Peckett 0-6-0ST (786/1899), a long time citizen of Cannock Chase. *Mike Wood*

Above:
The Chasewater Light Railway runs its preserved locomo-tives and stock on track bordering the large reservoir of that name at Chasetown, Staffordshire. Asbestos (Hawthorn Leslie 2780/1909) came from Turners Asbestos, Trafford Park, where it worked with partner Turnall near the Manchester Ship Canal, coming to Chasewater in 1968. The beautiful and rare Manchester, Sheffield & Lincolnshire Railway six-wheel brake dates from 1880, joining *Asbestos* from the Easingwold Railway. The delightful pairing was photographed on 9 July 1972. *Mike Wood*

Nuneaton to Lichfield

Above:
On 14 April 1962 Bescot's No 40646 was engaged by the SLS for a run to Bedford, Leamington Spa and Northampton. In poor weather conditions, the 4-4-0 was photographed at Nuneaton Abbey Street.

Below:
Inside-cylinder Peckett locomotives were a distinct rarity. Newdigate colliery's 0-6-0ST No 4 was built at Peckett's Bristol works, as works No 1787, in 1933. *Mike Wood*

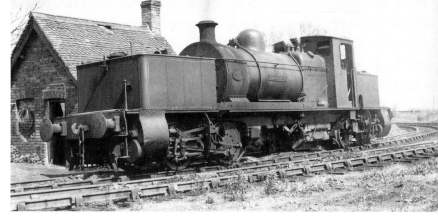

Very few Beyer-Garratt locomotives have worked in Britain and, as a result, Baddesley colliery's *William Francis* became very popular with railway photographers. The 0-4-4-0 was built by Beyer Peacock, as works No 6841, in 1937. *Jim Hardy*

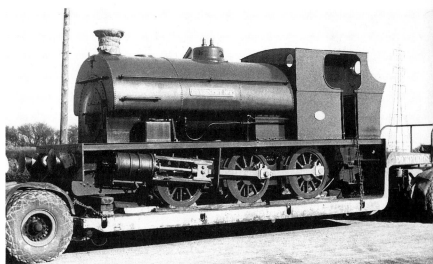

After a long period of service at Coventry colliery, *Coventry No 3* was taken by Pickfords low loader to Birch Coppice colliery, near Tamworth, for an extension to its working life. *Mike Wood*

Baddesley colliery's rail outlet for coal was via exchange sidings near the main Trent Valley line north of Atherstone, but having to cross the important A5 trunk road en route. *William Francis* was stained by limescale insolubles from leaks beneath the dome cover at it was pictured crossing the main road under the control of the fireman's red flag. *Mike Wood*

Left:
Avonside 0-4-0ST No 1386 of 1897 went new to Dunn & Shute, contractors at the town dock in Newport. It was later transferred to the Alexandra Dock & Railway Co on its establishment being taken over by the GWR and becoming GWR No 1340. *Trojan* was sold by the GWR to the Victoria Colliery Co of Wellington, Shropshire, and saw service at their collieries before going to Alders paperworks, Tamworth, when withdrawn from Church Gresley colliery. The locomotive left Alders in 1968, being preserved by John True at Didcot.
Jim Hardy

Left:
Trojan's companion at Alders was an Andrew Barclay 0-6-0ST (1576/1918), officially known as 'Guzzling Gertie'. It was supplied new to Nobels Explosives, Glasgow, and sent to Pembrey, Glamorgan, before going to Alders in 1927. Fitted with spark-arresting chimney, she was reboilered in 1947 and finally scrapped in 1957.
Mike Wood

Left:
No 44752, fitted with Caprotti valve gear and Timken roller bearings, was one of seven Class 5s so introduced in 1948 (Nos 44748-54). No 44752 was photographed piloting a 'normal' Class 5 on a Euston-Manchester express at Lichfield Trent Valley. It is sad that many main line signalboxes have disappeared, their distinctive bell codes and the falling 'clang' of pegs being heard no more due to the introduction of automatic signalling systems and area power boxes. *J. W. Ellson*

Above:
The unique prototype 'Royal Scot' rebuild No 46170 was built in December 1929 as the high-pressure experimental locomotive No 6399 *Fury*. It was rebuilt with a non-standard prototype taper boiler in November 1935. The boiler was shortened for series production. This superb shot of *British Legion* hard at work and in dirty condition was captured on film between Handsacre and Lichfield on a heavy express (W270). It was also unique in having a Stanier-type cab since all other rebuilds retained Fowler cabs. As a confirmed 'Scot' devotee, the 'Legion' was the author's favourite.
J. W. Ellson

Below:
Overhead electrification at Rugeley added to the already tangled skies where high pylons took the energy produced at Rugeley 'A' and 'B' power stations to the National Grid. No D295 on a down Liverpool express greeted a clean No 45595 *Southern Rhodesia* at Rugeley working the 12.50 Sundays Only Barrow-Euston service (1A46). On withdrawal of all steam services, the 2,000hp Type 4s (later Class 40s) were to prove superb machines, if limited in horsepower with their non-intercooled 16SVT engines.

Left:
A final photograph of the pre-diesel, pre-electric era typified by a vigorous departure from Stafford by 'Crab' 2-6-0 No 42812 with a local for Crewe, freely exhausting to an open sky with thunderous staccato music in the age before the wires came and steam went. No 42812 was built in May 1929; it was withdrawn in June 1966.

Left:
The 'Duchesses' were quickly cut up after their mass withdrawal in 1964. They were, perhaps, an embarrassment as they could easily outperform the replacing diesels on the severe northern banks. Unsuited to the sharp curves and dubious track of freight yards, their passing was swift. No 46228 *Duchess of Rutland* rapidly succumbed to the cutter's torch at Cashmores of Great Bridge.

Left:
Steam returned to the West Midlands on 12-14 November 1993 when preserved 'Austerities' *Whiston* and *Wimblebury* came from Foxfield to Littleton colliery to work merry-go-round empties over the steeply-graded line. Steve Turner's *Whiston* posed for a 'night' photographic session at the colliery on the 14th before returning home. Within days Littleton was doomed. The colliery closed on 10 December 1993. Disgusting! But await further developments.